DANNY DANZIGER has written fifteen books on a range of diverse subjects, including *We Are Soldiers* and *The Year 1000*, which went to number one and stayed on the bestseller list for seven months. Danny's weekly interview column 'Best of Times, Worst of Times', won many accolades and awards over twelve years.

SUB

**Real Life on Board with the
Hidden Heroes of the Royal
Navy's Silent Service**

DANNY DANZIGER

sphere

SPHERE

First published in Great Britain in 2011 by Sphere
This paperback edition published in 2012 by Sphere

A CIP catalogue record for this book
is available from the British Library.

ISBN 978-0-7515-4593-7

Typeset in Bembo by M Rules
Printed and bound in Great Britain by
Clays Ltd, St Ives plc

Papers used by Sphere are from well-managed forests
and other responsible sources.

MIX
Paper from
responsible sources
FSC® C104740

Sphere
An imprint of
Little, Brown Book Group
100 Victoria Embankment
London EC4Y 0DY

An Hachette UK Company
www.hachette.co.uk

www.littlebrown.co.uk

For Diana

CONTENTS

CONTENTS

SUB

INTRODUCTION

It was the best of times, it was the worst of times.

I remember looking at a sparkling sea as I walked along the beach at Aldeburgh in Suffolk before joining HMS *Torbay*, and being completely unable to imagine actually living *under* the water.

Nevertheless, it was going to happen: in a week's time I'd be flying up to Faslane in Scotland to join HMS *Torbay*, a hunter-killer Trafalgar-class nuclear submarine.

Since childhood, I had always dreamed about going on a submarine. As a writer, I wanted to write about the crew who live and work under the oceans and have such a unique and challenging working life, and now my request to write about life on a submarine had been granted by the Royal Navy and the Ministry of Defence. But, to tell the truth, I was nervous. Three weeks on a nuclear submarine may seem a small challenge compared with the consecutive months these submariners spend under the oceans, but I sensed it would be a testing time for me.

The first challenge I encountered was at the quayside. It had never occurred to me how you get into a submarine. What, and where would you imagine the entrance to be? A door at the side? A submarine has no doors. A window or porthole of some sort? A submarine has no windows or viewing platform on to the outside world, so once submerged, don't imagine you will have a scuba-like view of beautiful corals and interesting sea life. Give up? Take the gangplank to the casing, turn right to the back end of the fin and climb up to the main access hatch. Ease yourself on to a ladder, which takes you straight down until you reach a small platform. Keep circling until you find another ladder, which changes direction forty-five degrees, and plunges down again. At the bottom of that, you can either turn left into the reactor compartment or right forward to the control room, depending on your destination. Oh, and don't bring a suitcase, it would never make it down the hatch.

HMS *Torbay* has five decks and is around 85 by 10 by 10 metres; as a comparison, a London double-decker bus is 10 by 5 by 3 metres, and a football pitch is 100 metres long. The Navy's Vanguard-class submarines (which carry Trident missiles) are a comparatively spacious 150 metres long. The Astute class, which will ultimately replace

Trafalgar-class submarines, is also significantly larger, but requires fewer crew to operate due to the advanced technology and automated systems on board (it's also quieter than its predecessors, operates the most advanced sonar system in the world, and is the first Royal Navy submarine not to have a traditional periscope, instead using electro-optics to capture a 360-degree image of the surface). So all in all, I was about to experience life at the grittier end of the service.

Inside the submarine, the passageways are narrow, the ceilings low, and numerous valves and pipes and ancillary pieces of machinery swoop low enough to give a sharp reminder of their presence if you are not prescient enough to duck. There is a constant hissing sound from the various pipes and the corridors are illuminated by an unwaveringly pitiless high-wattage fluorescent light.

There are 125 submariners on board, all dressed in naval number fours, dark-blue heavy canvas trousers with a myriad of outer pockets, and a blue cotton shirt. In my civilian gear, I looked as conspicuous as a visitor from outer space as everyone bustled past me, open-mouthed to see a civilian wandering around on board – but no one had time to stop and chat; setting sail is one of the busiest times for a submarine.

Someone advised me to go to the wardroom, which is where the officers are based, and, happy to have a place to hang out, I made my way to Two Deck. The only furniture was three wooden tables, each with benches, the walls decorated with photographs of ancient underwater vessels, plus photographic portraits of the Queen and Prince Philip taken, I would guess, two or three decades ago.

Cups of tea were offered, introductions made, and I was invited back up the ladders to watch the departure from the bridge with the Captain and the Executive Officer (XO).

It had been a warm spring weekend – warm for southwest Scotland anyway – and Gareloch was calm and still as two tugs pulled us away from the quay, necessary because a submarine is difficult to manoeuvre on the surface in tight waters. A submarine has no keel, so if there's any roughness on the surface, the boat (and a submarine is always a boat, not a ship) rolls in a unique and sick-making manner.

When the submarine is free from any hazards and pointing in the right direction, the Captain tells the XO, his number two, to let go of the tugs and then the submarine starts propelling on the surface under her own steam, down Faslane Bay, through the Rhu Narrows and into the Firth of Clyde, sheltered from the Atlantic Ocean by the Kintyre Peninsula, with the tugs just standing by to assist if need be.

Eventually we make it to the open sea and the Captain gives the order, 'Dive the submarine,' and a few moments later someone says over the intercom, 'Diving now, diving now.'

As I clamber down the vertiginous ladders of the main access hatch again, I take a last deep gulp of fresh air as the hatch is closed, and a few minutes later we slip under the waters.

Actually, there is very little movement once we're under the water: no rolling, no pitching and, unless you looked at the depth dial to verify your depth, you could be 10 metres, 100 metres or 20,000 leagues under the sea.

Dinner is a friendly affair. The twenty-two officers are mostly in their twenties and thirties, and it's clear they are close. The banter, which I remember from researching my book on the Army, is still there, but it is more affectionate. The captain is served his dinner by the leading steward and, as he likes to dine at 8 p.m., a frosted glass appears at 7.59, and on the hour a Coca-Cola is ceremoniously poured into the glass. There is absolutely no alcohol on board, a rule that exists on every Royal Navy vessel. I would describe the standard of cuisine as superior school food; in fact, many of the dishes seem eerily similar to the culinary repertoire of my own.

A submarine never sleeps. The entire boat is divided into two watches; everyone works six hours on and six hours off, so unless you get to sleep immediately after your watch, which is unlikely, you're going to be averaging a lot less sleep than six hours, which makes it a very exhausting gig.

I was anxious to see my accommodation. It turned out that I had been allocated the weapons stowage compartment, or Bomb Shop, as the place where I would be sleeping. Compared to the alternative of 'the racks', this was considered spacious – I was being given upgraded accommodation. A metal pallet with one thin blanket folded on top was to be my bed – no sheets, no chocolate mint resting on the pillow, indeed no pillow. And, on either side of the bed, which was literally wedged between them, were stacks of Spearfish torpedoes, and even bigger Tomahawk land-attack missiles, each so close I could reach out and cuddle one during the night. I thought a practical joke was being played on me. This was a particular kind of hell, and I could only react in one way – no way.

And so I found my eventual resting place on board. The racks. These are small – very small – and narrow bunks, piled three high in a pitch-dark compartment and, believe me, there is no dark darker than the part of a submarine that has no lights. The smell of the racks, with around eighty men arranged around them, was unique, but in the awful, hideous range I mean, not scented and fragrant. (Although after a few days I ceased to notice it.)

There were metal hooks on which to hang your clothes.

As people came back off shifts, they would hang their uniforms over the last lot. So when you got up, you could only feel for your clothes and hope you had the right set: for me it was the feel of a tape recorder in the trouser pocket and a notepad in the shirt pocket that enabled me to distinguish my clothes at all.

I had the plum middle bunk, which was enough to necessitate a sort of swallow dive to secure entrance, and then a silent prayer that one remained lodged there throughout the night. The fellow above me fell out of his rack on my second night, and sometimes I imagine I can still hear that awful thud and his puzzled, sleep-sozzled cry of pain as he landed.

The heads – naval term for loos – were one deck above and, again it required a steep vertical climb up a metal ladder, at the same time balancing toothbrush, razor, towel, etc. Shower? I was told not to have 'a Hollywood' – submarine slang for an over-long, self-indulgent, waste of precious water. The shower etiquette on a submarine is as follows: brief burst of water to moisten body, turn off water. Soap or shampoo, if desired, turn on water to wash off suds, turn off water as soon as possible. A submarine makes its own water but not copious amounts, so everyone is rightfully parsimonious with water consumption. After a while in this all-male boat, I came to the conclusion there was little point in showering at all, which was enormously liberating. Furthermore, wearing a naval uniform and looking the same as everyone else further highlighted the pointless vanity of daily ablutions.

It took me a day to find somewhere I could do my interviews. In the end someone suggested a storage room in the most forward part of the boat, and although it took an elaborate and slightly embarrassing dance to wedge my interviewee and myself into that small hole, it became a wonderful office space.

And so I spent the days – or were they nights? (Because soon time had no relevance) – interviewing officers and sailors, getting to know these men who spend up to three hundred days of the year away from wives and girlfriends and parents and children, fresh air and sunshine, their homes and their country.

In the end, the original allotted time of three weeks at sea became nearer two weeks, as *Torbay* was re-tasked to go on a secret mission. As a civilian, my presence was now not required, so I had to be let off at the nearest port.

I was sad to say goodbye. Everyone on the boat had shown me great kindness, plus the unique environment made it an experience I'll remember for ever. It was testing to live without communications with nearest and dearest, and, with no exercise, and three hearty meals a day, plus constant access to the nutty basket (see glossary), I put on nearly a stone, a legacy that still remains . . .

INTRODUCTION

The Submarine Service has traditionally been known as the Silent Service, but I hope these interviews will serve to introduce and personalise a group of men who heroically do a difficult, dangerous and demanding job in physically uncomfortable and challenging conditions, and don't always get the recognition and acclaim they deserve.

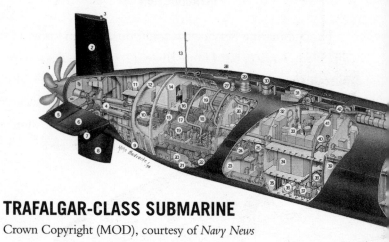

TRAFALGAR-CLASS SUBMARINE

Crown Copyright (MOD), courtesy of *Navy News*

Key

1. Propeller
2. Upper rudder segment
3. Aft anchor light
4. Rudder and hydroplane actuating rods
5. Starboard hydroplane
6. Horizontal stabiliser
7. Circulating water inlet, condenser cooling
8. Lower rudder segment
9. Retractable secondary propulsion motor
10. Rudder and hydroplane hydraulic actuators
11. Aft ballast tanks
12. Hull aft pressure dome
13. Portable ensign staff
14. Technical office
15. Propeller drive shaft thrust block and flexible coupling
16. Emergency propulsion motor
17. Combining gearbox
18. Main turbines
19. Turbo generators
20. Lubricating oil tank
21. Pressure hull frames
22. Condenser
23. Feed tank
24. HP air compressor
25. Chilled water plants
26. Workshop
27. Capstan
28. Hinged cleats
29. Engine room hatch
30. Aft escape hatch
31. Towed buoy
32. Watertight bulkhead, typical
33. Manoeuvring room
34. Switchboard room
35. Hydrogen storage bottles
36. Air treatment unit
37. AC/DC motor generator
38. Diesel generators
39. Reactor compartment
40. Main steam valve
41. Diesel engine exhaust duct
42. Towed buoy winch
43. Exhaust muffler
44. Main access hatch
45. Commanding officer's cabin
46. Cooling tank
47. Diesel oil tank
48. Air purification plant
49. Junior ratings' mess
50. Air system main supply fan

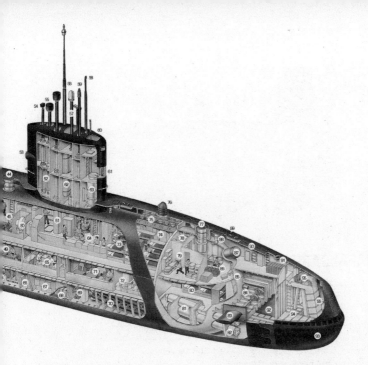

51. Mast well
52. Mast hydraulic actuators
53. Aft sonar
54. Diesel exhaust
55. Snort induction mast, fresh air
56. Communications antennae masts
57. Radar mast
58. Attack periscope
59. Search periscope
60. Surface navigation position
61. Forward sonar
62. Diesel fuel-oil expansion tank
63. Conning tower access
64. Control room
65. Galley
66. Garbage ejector compartment
67. Data distribution racks
68. Battery compartment
69. Torpedo handling gear
70. Weapons stowage compartment
71. Senior ratings' mess
72. Junior ratings' bathroom
73. Senior ratings' bunks

74. Sonar equipment room
75. Hull sonar glands
76. Sonar housing
77. Forward escape hatch
78. Coxswain's stores
79. Dry provisions store
80. Junior ratings' bunks
81. Torpedo tubes
82. Torpedo tube bow caps
83. Retractable forward hydroplane
84. Hydroplane hydraulic actuator
85. Hull forward pressure dome
86. CO_2 absorption unit
87. Weapon embarkation hatch
88. Forward capstan
89. Hinged cleats
90. Removable casing plates
91. Retractable fairlead
92. Number 2 main ballast tank
93. Forward sonar housing
94. Anchor stowage and cable locker
95. Anchor windlass
96. Number 1 main ballast tank

INSIDE A TRAFALGAR-CLASS NUCLEAR SUB

The Trafalgar class is a hunter-attack submarine designed to dive deeper than three hundred metres and move faster than twenty knots. It is stealthy, versatile and lethal.

The layout of the submarine is easiest to understand if it's described as being split into five compartments. The first compartment is forward of 29 Bulkhead and houses one of the two submarine escape compartments and most of the sleeping area. The next compartment is the hotel services section, which has the control room, where you drive, navigate and fight the submarine, the sound room, from which the sonar is operated, the galley, separate mess areas for the officers, senior rates and junior rates, and, at the bottom, the weapon-stowage compartment (WSC), also known as the Bomb Shop. Aft of that is the ship's office.

Behind this is the reactor compartment, the heart of the submarine and home to the nuclear reactor. The reactor itself sits in a heavily shielded compartment, no bigger than an average wheelie bin, surrounded by pipework and viewable through a thick glass window. Aft of the reactor compartment is the manoeuvring room where the propulsion watch monitor the reactor and all associated systems; below this are the switchboard room and the diesel generators. In the final compartment is the engine room, where the bulky items of machinery – main engines, turbogenerators that produce electricity, gearbox – are housed, among other things.

Physically, the submarine can almost be divided in half at the control room. Everything forward of this is either a living, operating or fighting space (and sometimes a combination of more than one of these), whereas everything aft is related to propulsion spaces, with the reactor in the middle of it. From a personnel perspective, the ship's company of 120 persons is divided into four departments under the commanding officer: a warfare department (or branch), a marine engineering branch, a weapons engineering branch and a logistics branch, and there are four heads of departments, or HODs, that run those.

The warfare department operates and fights the submarine under the command of the executive officer. Experts at manning the sonar, they know what they're listening for, but also have control of the weapons and the systems that fire them. The sonar team builds a tactical picture, while the warfare officers navigate using numerous aids including the periscopes.

The weapons engineering department maintains all the equipment and weapons under the command of the weapons engineering officer. The Spearfish torpedoes and Tomahawk land-attack missiles (TLAM for short) carried by HMS *Torbay* are continuously monitored and, when necessary, are prepared for battle by engineering technicians in the Bomb Shop. The maintainers are mainly focused on the servicing and repair of the sonar, radar, navigational aids, communication equipment and the provision of electrical supply that feeds all the equipment. The department also includes a small number of radio operators or communications information system ratings.

Marine engineering is split between the nuclear watchkeepers and the personnel who look after the propulsion systems, fire-fighting equipment and hotel services. So some of the marine engineers are under the propulsion tab and also operate the laundry. In fact, virtually every one of the 130 people on board has a secondary and often a tertiary role, which is why it is not easy to define specifically what one person actually does, because the skills are mapped according to personalities as well as capabilities. For example, the leading steward, who serves the officers their meals on board, will also spend time on the planes actually steering the boat and, if someone gets injured, he has a tertiary role as a qualified first-aider. So he could have spent an hour on the planes, climbed off that to serve spaghetti bolognese on a Tuesday – it's always spag bol on a Tuesday – and, just as he's put the plate down, the alarm goes because someone's fallen down a hatch, and he races off to attend to them with first aid.

In logistics you have chefs, stewards, stores, and a branch called writers, who do administration. Logistics is responsible for food and food preparation, and ordering and supplying all the spares on board. Getting the logistics right first time is very important: you can't afford to run out of anything on a submarine, particularly if that submarine can't surface because it's in sensitive waters.

A nuclear submarine is, as you would expect, powered by the nuclear reactor, housed in the reactor compartment – the sealed, lead-lined compartment that sits roughly in the centre of the submarine. The entire purpose of the reactor is to produce heat, which converts water into steam that feeds the main engines for propulsion and the turbo-generators that produce the submarine's electricity, as well as being used in the distillation of sea water for drinking – all without the need for fresh air. Alongside the reactor itself are two large steam generators (effectively 'kettles') and a large maze of supporting pipework and pumps. The compartment is unmanned, and is only ever entered when the reactor is shut down during routine maintenance in harbour or in an emergency when at sea, which is extremely rare.

In the reactor is a collection of uranium-238 fuel elements that provide huge amounts of energy to power the vessel – equivalent to the amount of energy required to power a town. In uranium, as with a number of other chemical elements, the nucleus of an atom is just about stable. If a neutron is fired at the atom, the uranium becomes heavier and unstable and the atom splits, releasing energy that is used to produce steam by heating up water in the steam generators. As this reaction happens, another neutron is released, which goes on to pound another atom, until you get a chain reaction or 'fission', which is self-sustaining and exponential – and could cause an explosion in a microsecond if it wasn't kept in check. So there has to be a level of control on the reaction to prevent overheating and, to this end, control rods made of hafnium, which absorbs radiation, are inserted into the reactor core to absorb the excess neutrons.

The heat produced in the reactor heats pressurised water (the primary coolant) to a temperature far higher than its normal boiling point, which is run via pipes and pumps into the steam generator and then back to the reactor in a closed circuit, more commonly known as the 'primary circuit'. This heat from the primary-coolant pipework is used to heat up a body of water outside the tubes in the steam generator. That steam is passed through a number of turbines, some of which drive the sub around on its propulsor (propeller), and some of which supply electricity, which then runs everything else on the submarine. So the fission process is using a nuclear reaction to create heat, to create steam, to turn turbines and to make propulsion and electricity.

The reactor and its associated systems are monitored by the manoeuvring-room team. There are five people on each watch in manoeuvring who systematically monitor a large number of gauges, dials and switches that control numerous pumps, hull valves and, of course, the systems associated with the reactor. The reactor-panel operator, or RPO, monitors the reactor core and controls the hafnium rods to increase or decrease the reactivity. Seated next to him is the junior member of the team, the throttle control-panel operator, who controls the throttles on the main engines, responding to engine orders from the control room. Next to him is the electrical-panel operator, who controls the downstream electrical systems to ensure the generation of electricity is happening as it should. These three are in turn monitored by the nuclear warrant officer and the engineering officer of the watch and, with further support from engineering, the watch is always eight strong, and can call on others if they need to.

The submarine is run from the control room. This is where you drive the submarine, navigate it, fight it, and command the propulsion systems. The room has a host of sophisticated electrical equipment, pipework, communications systems and control panels. The periscopes are perhaps what submarines are most associated with. The position in the boat of the control room is determined by where the periscopes are, because of the importance of the captain being able to see out during an attack, particularly in the close-up battles of the past. In the Trafalgar-class submarine, there are two periscopes: search and attack. Each compliments the other with numerous different functions that include provision of a television feed, high magnification for looking at long-range shipping and a thermal-imaging function for low lighting conditions. Although they do have an intelligence-gathering function, the reality is that the periscopes aren't used very much now, apart from ensuring ship safety – the old days of fighting a submarine from the periscope are long gone.

When he is ready to take the periscope up, the captain will order the systems panel operator to raise whichever periscope he wants, with the words 'Raise search' – the term 'up periscope' is very much a creation of the movies. The periscope will start coming up, and then the periscope watch-keeper will grab the handles as it's coming up, and when he's happy with the height of it, he will start rotating

19

it. And when he's finished, he'll put the handles up and say, 'Lower search', and it'll go all the way down.

When at periscope depth, which means the submarine is lying just below the surface of the water, it's in quite a dangerous position, because it can't be seen by anybody else, and if it got hit full on by a merchant vessel – that could cut a submarine in two. So at periscope depth the periscope watch-keeper must ensure there are no merchant vessels, or any other vessel for that matter, that are likely to hit the submarine.

The watch keeper will rotate 360 degrees at roughly two rotations a minute. He'll start off in low power, conducting a 360-degree sweep of the outside world. He will then switch to high power and look through a 200-degree arc before switching back to low power to conduct another 360-degree sweep. This means he can look in the water immediately around the boat as well as scanning further afield. While looking out, he will focus his lens with only one third of the circle looking at the sea and the remaining two thirds concentrating on the sky to look for potential air threats. Despite HMS *Torbay*'s advanced sonar, there are a few occasions when quiet warships or 'bow blanking' merchant ships are not detected by the sound room, so the periscope might be the only sensor that detects their presence. The officer manning the periscope will then pass on any information into the overall tactical picture.

To use a periscope effectively, you need to have the lighting within the boat at a level that's consistent with what's happening above the water. In daytime, you can have fairly bright lighting in the control room, but if you want to see out of the periscope at night, then your eyes need to be adjusted for night vision, which means that there will be reduced lighting.

During conflicts in the past – similar to those in the John Mills war films – torpedoes were straight-running, and not equivalent to today's wire-guided counterparts. That meant the captain had to approach the target in close confines to be sure of success, and the entire engagement was controlled by the captain's accurate calculations from the periscope. These skills are still regularly practised and, while they are not used for a close-range attack, they are equally important when trying to manoeuvre the submarine into the optimum intelligence-gathering position. However, Astute-class submarines, the first of which was launched in 2007, have non-hull penetrating electro-optical masts. These have much improved optics and provide a 360-degree picture recorded by a TV camera; this is immediately reviewed on a screen after the mast is lowered, reducing the time the mast is exposed. Every bit of information that the commanding officer needs comes into the control room, so there are many screens. There are screens showing where the submarine is, relative to the seabed and to other ships, which receive their information from the sound room, where all the sonar is coming from. Information can be fed in from the periscopes, and from intelligence, via radio, all contributing to a picture of where the submarine is in relation to everything else. When the search periscope is raised, the navigational aids are updated by GPS, similar to a car satnav; however, when deep, the submarine's estimated position is calculated using tidal-stream predictions with accurate recordings of the submarine's speed and log. The navigation section feeds information on the submarine's position to different equipment that would be used during an attack. And the captain uses the same information to drive the submarine around the oceans, bearing in mind that, apart from when he's got a periscope raised, he can't see where he is going.

The control room is also a massive communications hub that can talk to every area of the submarine. At its port aft end is the communications office or WT office (which refers to the wireless telegraphy used in the Second World War). Here the communications ratings monitor the submarine broadcast – a passive method of receiving intelligence, orders, updates or administrative traffic. They also prepare messages or 'signals' for transmission when at periscope depth, or set up equipment to talk to other shipping using a variety of differing means. The days of flag-waving or bunting have gone; communications for a modern submarine are pretty complex, ranging from all forms of satellite communications, which can be UHF (ultra-high frequency), EHF (extra-high frequency), SHF (super-high frequency) or VHF (very high frequency), down to very low-frequency waves, which you can only receive just below the surface.

On a 'sneaky' patrol – i.e. one doing intelligence collection – a submarine won't communicate at all for six weeks, but it will receive information once or twice a day from headquarters, updating it on the latest intelligence, providing it with news on what's going on in the rest of the world and providing administrative support. That's normally received by satellite in quite short bursts when at periscope depth. Nothing comes across in plain voice: it's all double encrypted, so it can't be intercepted and understood by others. And perhaps just as important to the crew is the communicator's ability to manage and repair the submarine's computer network, which affects whether or not emails and messages from home are received.

At the port forward end of the control room is the ship's control console, where a team of three drives the submarine and operates its systems. The planesman sits in front of depth, speed and attitude gauges while operating a control column – very similar to an aircraft. The one-man control column is used to operate the small fore-planes in the bows of the submarine and the larger after-planes located near the rudder. When ordered, the planesman changes the depth of the submarine by pulling or pushing the column, while by moving the wheel left or right he alters the ship's heading to port or starboard.

Next to the planesman is the panel operator, or simply 'Panel'. Supervised by a technical senior rate, Panel controls the movements of all masts and the operation of the hull valves that either bring in water or dispel it to alter the weight or 'ballast' of the submarine. He also controls the movement of water between internal tanks to ensure the submarine remains level or 'in trim'. Essentially, a submarine is like a cigar tube with ballast tanks forward and aft. When the submarine is on the surface, the ballast tanks are full of air to keep it buoyant. To dive, Panel opens the main vents, which are large brass plugs sitting on top of the ballast tanks, air is expelled and water enters the tanks, making the submarine heavy. She dives with the help of the water in the tanks and her propulsion driving her further down. To surface, Panel makes sure the main vents are shut and, when ordered, he operates the blow valves, which puts high-pressure air into the ballast tanks to expel the water and make the submarine quasi buoyant for surface operations. These high-pressure air systems are critical, so Panel monitors them all.

The final party of the control team is the ship control officer of the watch, or 'Ship Control', who's trained to make sure the planesman and panel operator are working together. He relays orders to dive and surface the submarine, relays speed information to the engineers back aft, and is the centre point of the communications to the whole boat. He's critical, because the planesman and Panel simply do what they're told – Ship Control is the person who uses his initiative to get the submarine doing what the captain wants it to do. And he will react if something's not happening. So he's trained in standard operating procedures, SOPs for short, which determine how the submarine runs normally, and in emergency operating procedures (EOPs), which is what happens if something goes wrong, and he's the person who makes that first broadcast, which is called a 'pipe' in the Navy. If there's an emergency, he's the person who takes the initial actions and starts the emergency recovery.

Submarines are inherently unnatural – operating in the most unforgiving of environments, their fundamental problem is that they are under water. There are many potential emergencies because a submarine is a complex machine, so the list of things that can go wrong is never ending.

The most dangerous is a flood; most submarines that have been lost over the years, particularly during World Wars I and II, were lost due to floods, although these were usually due to some breach caused by hitting something or being hit by something. Consequently, a flood is one of the few emergencies where a submarine will surface rather than staying dived. There are places you can't surface, like under the ice caps, and maybe some ultra-sensitive areas but, apart from those, the reaction to a flood is to surface, because if there's a breach of the hull, you can relieve the amount of water coming in by surfacing and reducing the pressure so you can control the flood.

Fire is next on the danger list. Being in an enclosed environment, even a small fire can generate a significant amount of acrid smoke and the consequence of that is you'll soon run out of air. So putting out the fire as soon as possible and returning the atmosphere to a breathable condition is of paramount importance.

You can also have a mechanical failure: the planes could jam and you're suddenly heading downwards towards the sea bottom, or heading upwards to the surface and, potentially, a collision with a ship. Or you could have a nuclear failure, where the nuclear reactor shuts down: there's no danger to people from that, but if you suddenly lose your heat source, that means you stop producing electricity and suddenly you're reliant on a comparatively small battery, which can only last so long.

There are some high-pressure systems in the boat, both air and hydraulic oil, which can fracture. The danger of high-pressure escaping air could cause fragments to hit people, but also, that air is needed for breathing or for surfacing the submarine, so you don't want to lose it. If the hydraulic oil system bursts, there's an inherent risk of fire. Electrical malfunction will also give you a loss of control.

In general, therefore, nothing in a submarine is reliant on one system. Each will have a number of back-up systems with alternative sources of energy supply; for example, something using electricity will have an alternative electricity supply or, in the case of hull valves, air or hydraulics. In an extreme situation, some systems can be operated manually.

In the forward starboard side of the control room is the tactical systems area known as 'ops'. Here, the command system collates all the most current information from sensors and outstations to produce a tactical picture that is manageable and easy to interpret for the captain. The tactical picture is used for spatial awareness, so the submarine can remain undetected and unharmed by moving away from vessels. Everyone has right of way over a submarine because they don't know you're there, so when you're under water, you have to keep out of other people's way. Next to them is fire control, for activating the torpedoes and cruise missiles.

A torpedo is essentially a big bit of explosive in a cigar tube with an electric motor; it dispenses a thin wire so it remains attached to the submarine for tens of miles. In the old days you would have to guess where the target was going to be when the torpedo got to the end of its run, and fire in anticipation of that, and if the target then altered course once you'd fired, there was nothing you could do about it, apart from fire another torpedo. With a wire-guided torpedo, the submarine remains connected with the torpedo, and whatever the target does, you just direct the torpedo to follow it. You get the torpedo close to where the ship is, then the torpedo's own mini-sonar detects the ship and homes in, and there's nothing the ship or submarine you're attacking can do at that point.

If you want to sink a ship or another submarine you need a torpedo. If you want to attack something on land you need a cruise missile, or Tomahawk land-attack missile (TLAM).

The TLAM is an unmanned aerial bomb that has a range in excess of a thousand miles. It has a very sophisticated guidance system in it that takes GPS and other input, allowing it to attack targets very accurately. Give it a position, and you can almost stipulate which door you want it to go through. Or, to put it another way, you could fire it from Gibraltar and direct it to fly between the hallowed posts at Twickenham.

The weapons are stored in the weapons stowage compartment, colloquially known as the Bomb Shop. The Bomb Shop has all of the torpedoes and cruise missiles ready to be loaded and, invariably, submarines will go round with some of them already loaded into the tubes, ready to fire. There is a crew of weapons-engineering technicians who are maintaining those torpedoes, and load them on and off the submarine when she's in port.

The programming for the cruise missiles all happens on the same consoles as the torpedo; you just select 'cruise missile' not 'torpedo'. You then select the target and fire from the control room, not from the weapons stowage compartment, and it is the apocryphal red button with the word 'FIRE' on it that you press, and that's how you discharge a torpedo or a cruise missile.

In front of the periscopes and sandwiched between the ship control team and the tactical system operators is the captain's chair. From here the captain has access to his outstations and has a good 360-degree view of information that is critical for submarine safety or to attack a target. In peacetime open-ocean operations at periscope depth there will be twelve people on watch in the control room, all led by an officer of the watch or 'watch-leader', who positions the submarine as directed by the captain's instructions. When on patrol or when prosecuting a target, the control-room numbers grow to eighteen. A control room is a calm place to be 95 per cent of the time, but it will get noisier when a major change is about to happen, like the sub is about to surface or dive, and if there's an emergency, the excitement level rises very quickly. But when a submarine is doing what it's supposed to be doing, you'll generally get people quietly and calmly going about their business.

Forward of the control room is the sound room, which is home to all the sonar equipment – the ears of the submarine. With a mass of screens and headsets, the twelve sonar operators on watch use a number of different sonars linked to hydrophones, transducers and arrays around the submarine to listen to the outside world and piece together information to feed the tactical systems picture. The information received in the sound room is the principal means of working out who else is around in the ocean, and if you can see your enemy you're probably too close – it's much better to attack an enemy at arm's length.

Trafalgar-class submarines have the world's most advanced passive sonar system. It detects all the very many noises that the ocean makes, whether it be from the ocean itself, or from the animals that live in the ocean, things like shrimp and whales or dolphins – living sounds are termed biological, or 'bio' for short – plus the man-made sounds caused by other ships or, potentially, other submarines. If the noise is in the audible range, you'll be able to put on a pair of headphones and hear the sound of the propellers going around, or whatever machinery has been detected, and the sonar operator analyses the sound and tells you which direction it's going in and, if it's a ship, how fast it's going and what type of vessel it is.

Most merchant, fishing and cargo vessels have propulsion in the audible range: fishing vessels are not in the business of being quiet and stealthy, so they'll have chunky, fast-turning propellers, which will be quite noisy and clanky. Fishing vessels are generally quite easy to identify because you will hear the sound of the nets as well. To give some perspective, a submarine operating off Land's End can detect a ship leaving Bristol and, as it approaches, the sonar operators are able to determine the number of shafts the ship has and also the number of blades on each shaft. They can also determine the ship's speed and also the type of ship they are listening to.

Finally, the intensity of the contact (loud, moderate or faint) may give an indication of its range from the submarine. If it's outside the audible range, there's a computer screen showing a trace of that inaudible noise on it and how intense it is, and you'll then know the direction it's coming from. The trace might tell you a bit about what platform it's coming from, depending on the frequency. So when the trace appears but can't be heard, it is called through to the control room over the internal communications circuit or 'command line' by declaring, 'Ops controller, passive has a new contact on a bearing of X.' The only thing you will know is the direction or, rather, the bearing the noise is coming from, but you can deduce a lot from that alone. For example, the bearing will change depending on how you and the target are moving in relation to each other: a steady bearing means you're probably on a collision course and action will be required to avoid the contact. The captain and his team use the rate at which the bearing changes plus some clever mathematics to determine the range of the vessel and calculate its course and speed, which are all that is required to feed the torpedo its information for an attack.

A submarine is teeming with ancillary machinery just to support life, and the propulsion department looks after all that. You've got a whole series of machines that run high-pressure systems like hydraulic oil and high-pressure air, and electrics that run the submarine. You've got gear that keeps people alive: air-purification equipment that makes oxygen, carbon-dioxide scrubbers, carbon-monoxide burners, and all the computer equipment that keeps that right, and you've got machinery that makes fresh water both to drink and for the nuclear system.

Everybody on board a submarine knows something about all aspects of the sub, because to qualify as a submariner every sailor has to take an examination covering every aspect of submarine life. So no matter whether you're a steward, a propulsion guy, a warfare officer or a weapons expert, you have to go around the whole submarine and learn the different systems that make the submarine work, and the different roles everyone has. When you pass that test then you'll win the dolphins that you pin onto your number-one uniform. And the importance of that is if something goes wrong, like there's a fire, or a flood, or a high-pressure system bursts and you're the nearest person who can deal with an emergency, you've been trained to stop it getting worse: isolate the system, isolate the flood, put out the fire. It doesn't matter what your trade is – you can deal with the problem and live to fight another day.

COMMANDER ED AHLGREN OBE

As Commanding Officer of HMS *Torbay*, Cdr Ahlgren is charged with the responsibility and safety of the submarine and 163 staff, while ensuring strategic tasking is met at the tactical level.

I first went down in a submarine when we still had diesel boats and I must admit I didn't enjoy that at all – it was very close confines and had this distinctive oily, metallic smell, with people bumping into each other every five minutes. They had osmosis plants, by which you supposedly got fresh water from sea water, but they were never very efficient, so more often than not all you got was a bowl of water in which to wash your private areas, your hair was always greasy and your fingernails were always black, and your pores just soaked up the diesel and muck. I remember first time back home it took me two or three baths to get rid of the dirt and most of the afternoon to clean the tidemark off around the bath. As for the laundry – that was relegated either to a professional launderette or disposal!

I was next appointed as the communications officer in a Resolution-class ballistic submarine, which was designed to carry Polaris, the nuclear deterrent of the day before Trident. There were four of them, *Renown*, *Repulse*, *Resolution*, and *Revenge*, and their systems were totally different from diesel boats because they were nuclear, so you had to learn about nuclear weapon systems as well as nuclear reactors and a completely different propulsion train. When these boats went out on patrol they very rarely, if at all, came up to periscope depth, because if you put a mast up, someone could find you, and their whole *raison d'être* was to be out there, undetected, all of the time. We once spent eighty days under the sea and I didn't see daylight once in those eighty days, although I did return lighter, more pallid and with a healthy bank balance.

When I left that, I was lucky enough to serve on board HMS *Trafalgar* prior to my next career course. We always knew the Trafalgar class as 'shiny Ts', and it was like stepping into modern submarining. Everyone wanted a T-boat, as they went far afield on exciting missions – they were great – professionally challenging and thoroughly rewarding.

HMS *Torbay* was built in 1984, so OK, it is eighties technology, but she's fast, deep-diving, and has got a torpedo that can engage targets a dozen miles away, missiles that fly 1000 miles with precision accuracy, and she has got a sonar that picks up merchant vessels sixty to seventy miles away – it's one of the most advanced sonars in the world that is the envy of many. Also, we make our own oxygen, we can make electricity, we make our own water and we have got a reactor that could power the city of Plymouth. The only thing we really need is food and the ability to replenish any weapons we have expended. As far as handling, well, I tell you, when I am driving around the depths at fast speed and putting the angle on the boat and thoroughly enjoying myself, it's incredible and I have absolute pride in her.

There are bound to be poignant moments when you spend so long under the sea. I remember when Princess Diana passed away. We were on sea trials and doing our deep dive that day, but the captain spoke on Main Broadcast, which is unusual for a captain to do – it's either going to be really good news or really bad news, but either way it's something quite significant. And this came out: 'Princess Diana has been tragically killed in a tunnel in Paris.' The boat went very, very quiet and we had a moment of reflection ... How could she have died? She was in very good health and in the prime of her youth when we last sailed.

I was operations officer on board HMS *Triumph* on 11 September 2001. We were south of Iceland, participating in an anti-submarine exercise with American MPAs (maritime patrol aircraft) and we returned to periscope depth to receive a message: 'Owing to unforeseen circumstances, this exercise has been suspended.' We sat there for another hour, then, all of a sudden, a new SUBNOTE came in and we started going south at 20 knots, and then we knew something was amiss because we were meant to be going to Bergen, Norway for a run ashore. News started to filter through, because one of the chaps had a friend working in HQ who sent us some imagery and saw that commercial jets had flown into the Twin Towers. I remember thinking, somebody is having us on, as the enormity of the event was incredible.

We loaded more missiles in Crete, transited the Suez Canal, and out on down into the Indian Ocean. We then knew we were on our way to the Middle East and that we would probably be called forward for strike operations – very similar to the Gulf War, where a number of sub-marines were involved in strike operations. Mid-October we launched Tomahawk strikes into Afghanistan, although no one knew the targets except the captain and the weapons engineer, nor how many we were firing, which was probably for the best.

The captain would have been the only one who had the

full picture at that time, with a lot of high-grade intelligence coming through, although he can't tell just anybody for one reason or another, maybe protecting the intelligence source, or because something is time-critical.

As a commanding officer, I now get these signals coming in all the time, marked, 'Personal: for commanding officer' and it will all be encrypted and often I am the only person who reads it. But if we are going off on patrol, I will tell my boys as much about our future mission as I am able, within the confines of security regulation, as it gets everybody into the circle and promotes a feeling of trust, although I can't do that on the surface, because with mobile phones, Facebook and other media, you can no longer control what leaves a submarine and I can't take the risk that one of the boys will let it slip. It's only when I have dived and all the hatches are shut and clipped that I know I have absolute control on information flow.

Leading up to a strike, you will start receiving large amounts of signal traffic; it's an auditable trail and a timescale which starts about twenty-four hours before, basically, they tell you what your targets and mission packages are. And then the strike happens. There's no great hullabaloo or great big crescendo of activity, it is just so controlled and streamlined because we've practised that all the time at sea.

I have often wondered what Captain Wreford-Brown

must have felt when he sank the *Belgrano* in the Falklands; in those days it was very much up-close-and-personal, whites-of-your-eyes stuff, whereas with a TLAM strike the range can be up to 1000 miles. And even at the end of 1000 miles, these missiles are so precise – it's not a case of, 'Which building do you want me to hit?' It's, 'Which window do you wish me to fly it through?' They are extremely good weapons.

I am really, really fortunate because normally you will have just one submarine command but I have had two. I commanded HMS *Tireless* for two years. It was with immense trepidation I first joined *Tireless* and, after we both signed the control-room log, the other captain said, 'Well, it's yours now, there's the keys, you have command – look after her.' And I thought, Don't leave me! I remember sitting in my cabin, looking around, thinking, I'm the man in charge, I have got no one to turn to when I am at sea – all the decisions are mine and while I had been waiting seventeen years for this moment, it was still daunting. But my boys in *Tireless* were excellent, they truly were, and I moulded with the ship's company and had a fantastic, fulfilling two years.

Tireless went into extended maintenance for a year and its maintenance period was running longer than planned, so the decision was made to transfer me to a sister submarine, HMS *Torbay*.

Tradition is that when you are in command of a naval vessel you are accorded the honour of 'piping the side' as you go over the brow – the 'Bosun's Call', which is a low shrill-high shrill-low shrill sound that you would recognise from a Second World War black-and-white film. So the departing captain goes on board in the morning and gets piped on board. I arrived about half an hour later, and Darren Mason, my XO, met me in his best suit to say, 'Good morning, sir,' and escort me to the submarine. The previous captain then started the musters – we handed over items like the controlled drugs, including morphine, which is kept in a safe in my cabin, we had a few classified documents to hand over, various keys and, most importantly, he showed me how the PlayStation worked. Finally, we made a Main Broadcast pipe: 'Commander Ahlgren is now in command of HMS *Torbay*.' I signed the control-room log, we shook hands and I sat in my cabin as he went off – but, notably, he didn't get a pipe, as he was no longer in command, which I have often thought as quite brutal. The ship's company had fallen in and gave him three cheers. Oh, and he left sat resplendent on a torpedo on a trolley and, I thought, They are not doing that to me.

As poignant a moment as it is for a former CO, the ship's company wastes little time on nostalgia and gets on with normal business. I went into my Matstat brief (brief on the material state of the submarine), with my heads of department, who basically gave me a full rundown of their departments. The weapons engineering officer stated exactly what weapon load I had got on at the moment, the state of his department in terms of manpower, what repairs he was undertaking, what status of training he was at, and if he needed any call for specialised people. The marine engineer did the same; he told me the state of the reactor, what issues he had with his people, his training and sustainability, and the XO pretty much covered everything else, ranging from disciplinary issues, compassionate cases, routine administration . . . the list is endless.

After that we went for lunch and in the afternoon I separately met the junior rates mess and the senior rates mess followed by the wardroom, just to give them a flavour of what I wanted from them. I have seen some captains go on for hours about all sorts of things, but truth of the matter is – and it is very personal – all they want to know is what kind of guy you are and how you are going to lead them, therefore I try not to give them anything huge and grandiose which they are likely to forget as soon as you have exited the compartment. So I kept it quite short and sweet, ending with: 'I will play fair by you if you play fair by me.'

What truly makes a submarine and gives it its spirit are the people who live and breathe inside. My junior rates mess are fantastic; they live in the smallest compartment of the three with the most amount of people in it. These are the guys who make the submarine tick. When they are not engaged on their primary duty of operations, maintenance or support, they are doing the lifting, the shifting, the cleaning, the scrubbing out, but they generally see the good in everything and will find the humour in anything – nothing is ever safe and should you make that one faux pas, they will never let you forget it. Just a great set of guys to be around.

The senior rates are the managers of the submarine, who have the experience and the years served and, therefore, I tended to learn an immense amount from these people who have seen the problems or issues countless times before. Above them are the officers and you have to have good, effective officers if you are to succeed. A submarine will normally sail with twenty officers – there's me at the top, the XO, the MEO and the WEO who each run their departments, and the lieutenant commanders, lieutenants and the sub-lieutenants beyond that, who are unbelievably loyal and dedicated.

As an example, there was a memorable occasion with navigating officer Dean Ingram: what he has just done recently is a good example of that. We returned on Thursday, having been away for three months, and the plan was to have a spot of leave before going out again for two months. We were reunited with our families at about 19:00 on Thursday night but Friday I get a phone call that the navigator of HMS *Talent*, which was out in the Middle East, had to come home for compassionate reasons. The navigator's plot is rather taut at the moment and all the other submarines were lining up to go to sea, so the only option was Dean Ingram.

I actually scripted my telephone call because I thought this could be a difficult conversation: I am about to tell this chap, who has just been reunited with his wife after three months, 'Sorry sunshine, you are packing a bag and going again.' I caught him as he was in a taxi going out for dinner with his wife, plus his in-laws, who had just come over from abroad and only see him once a year. After initial pleasantries he must have been thinking, Please get to the point, as a captain hardly ever rings one of his officers for a social chat in the evening. I, too, felt that I needed to be brief: 'Here it is, Dean. *Talent* needs a navigator and there aren't many options. You need to know that you are in the frame for a possible redeployment.' I expected him to give me some sort of rebuttal. 'You've got to be kidding me, sir' or 'Is there nobody else?' That would have been normal. But the only thing I got back from him was, 'When do I go and how long will I be gone?'

My wife and I have been in that situation time and time again, so I understand what he was going through, but the way he accepted it was incredibly professional and very humbling.

That is the way of life I have lived for twenty years and I wouldn't change a thing, but it has its stresses and strains. I have got a very understanding wife – that's key in our business and you usually find they are the driving force. When I first started seeing Becci, she didn't know what being a submariner entailed. She would be asking me, 'When am I going to hear from you again?' 'I don't know.' 'Where are you going?' 'Not too sure about that.' There was complete uncertainty and I thought, Great, here goes another relationship. Time has educated her in the life of a submariner and she now knows that our programmes can be unstable and that we can often leave early and yet be home earlier or later depending on the scope of our operations. So far she has gone the distance and it's been absolutely fabulous.

I remember my wife visiting me in Fujairah, United Arab Emirates. We were at a hotel with the officers and having five days there before going away again. Some of the other wives had flown out and we hadn't seen our wives for so long. The hotel was fabulous, lovely weather, we were all stood there at a reception enjoying freedom again . . . The phone in my pocket went, and it was headquarters, who were very brief and succinct. 'The commander-in-chief wants you to sail early.' 'That's very funny,' I said, 'but no jokes tonight, please.' 'I'm being totally serious,' was the reply and I had to return to the submarine to find out more by secure means. Becci knew instantly. 'You're sailing early, aren't you?' And I had to say, 'Yes I am,' and then tell all the other officers, who were pretty good about it – as were the wives, although after we'd sailed, the girls ran up a huge hotel bill on our credit cards – which was great, they deserved it and it appeared that we were not going to need money for some time to come. Telling the ship's company was also a challenge. We were planning to have a large barbecue with our friends and family and had spent quite a bit of money on food and entertainment. I gathered them round and explained that we were going to sea earlier than planned and that I couldn't tell them why, but it was important and that it would probably be best if they limited their partying. True to form, there was no complaint, plenty of humour generally aimed at the direction of the UK.

A submarine can do so many different things; a submarine can be used for everything from strike operations to intelligence-gathering, to landing Special Forces or protecting a task group, it goes on and on and on. But we've got fewer submarines now than we've ever had and we have more jobs than we've ever had, and the two don't quite go together, so there is a high operational tempo at the moment. We're longer at sea and when you think you're getting back, you don't, you get extended. Or you think you are going to sail in two weeks and you go in a week. And that can have a huge impact on the submarine force and also our loved ones – it can be quite draining.

It is a job, it's a calling, because I tell you something, it is all-encompassing and you have to give up quite a bit for it. It takes you right across to the other side of the world, away from the things you love, and all those little nice things in life that people take for granted, like walking down a country road, fresh air, the sun on your face or the stars at night, well, we don't have any of that for weeks and months at a time. We get paid rather well for it, but some of the stuff we have to do and endure is very taxing and it is fair to say that we earn our pay.

But the men will never complain; they will always come back to the fact that we see soldiers putting their lives on the line for their country, there are guys in trenches out in Afghanistan being shot at, bombed and mortared, and you will get the utmost respect for those people from my submarine crew. We aren't putting ourselves in front of shot and shell every day, but we have our own personal issues to deal with, although you will find when it comes to a tough decision or some bad news, my people will always turn round and say, 'Well, it could be much worse,' and there is the inevitable black humour that follows. But let's not forget that we are operating a highly technical multimillion-pound piece of equipment in one of the most unforgiving of environments, far from support and far from home – each day is a challenge underwater.

For me, this is what I have done for twenty years and now I am about to do something completely different. I'll miss it; I know I will miss it enormously. I will miss the camaraderie. We talk a lot these days about ethos and team spirit and all those other great and glorious words they use in leadership dictionaries. But working with a bunch of professional and dedicated people who have a cracking sense of humour, where no one day is ever the same has been amazing. I'm immensely proud of leading and commanding those people – they make the world go round for me.

Imagine sitting around a dinner table. 'So, what do you do?' I have the immense privilege to be able to say, 'I am a captain of a nuclear submarine.' That's great, isn't it? Not everybody can be a captain of a nuclear submarine, and I am very proud of what I do.

Commander Ahlgren relinquished command of HMS Torbay *in summer 2010 and moved on to Staff College.*

It was with much sadness that I left the submarine on 23 July. The dates and leaving ceremony all altered, as I had to go up to London for briefings at the Ministry of Defence, so my leaving dinner went ahead without me. However, on my return to Plymouth, my wife wanted to go for a drink in the local pub, which was not well received by a tired and tetchy submarine captain. After a few cross words, I grudgingly went to the pub – and there was the entire wardroom (with the only exception being the duty officer). If they had wanted to make a statement or an impact, they did it! I was totally lost for words and very humbled by it all (and I also had to apologise profusely to Mrs A!). They had bought me a nice crystal decanter and six matching glasses with the submarine's crest engraved with the phrase 'There's only one wheel on his wagon', which pertains to a song I used to sing on the bridge when things weren't going well. Additionally, we always used to have problems with our CO_2 scrubbers emitting a particular smell, which used to drive me insane, and to ensure I could always reminisce, they bought me a lady's perfume atomiser filled with that god-awful smell to recreate the atmosphere. They also bought me a framed black-and-white picture of the submarine – a fabulous present; the boys from the galley gave me a pasta recipe book as they know I love pasta, and the marine engineers had spent six weeks working a piece of brass into a replica of the submarine, which now sits proudly in my living room. We then had an evening in the pub, which truly hurt the next morning.

The fateful 23rd arrived, and it was with a heavy heart

that I returned on board for my last hour before I handed the boat over. Tradition stretching back to Nelsonian days has it that the captain is rowed ashore by his officers, and the boys lined the jetty and I was directed down some steps to a boat, which took me on a tour of the harbour before returning past the submarine where the boys gave me three cheers. I remember thinking, I'll bet Nelson didn't wear a lifejacket over his best uniform, though, but I guess times have changed. As I climbed the steps there was more to come – at the end of a ceremonial line of sailors was a Bentley to take me home with a bottle of champagne in the back – all paid for by the ship's company. I was overwhelmed, proud, sorry to be leaving, and a whole range of other emotions as I realised that potentially my submarine time was up.

LIEUTENANT COMMANDER MARK ALDER
Marine Engineering Officer

Lt Cdr Alder is responsible for the safe operation of the nuclear reactor and the propulsion system. Like his deputy and assistant engineer officers, he is an EOOW (engineering officer of the watch), keeping watches in the manoeuvring room. Alder is also responsible, as the head of the marine engineering department, for the management of the department's people, equipment and administration.

I'm the marine engineering officer responsible for provision to Command; essentially propulsion services and ship domestic services and maintaining the notice for sea. So if we're told, 'Right. You're going to sail in forty-eight hours,' we sail in forty-eight hours.

I'm supported by a team of warrant officers, chiefs and petty officers – seventy-two people in all. Everything that supports propulsion is our preserve, basically, everything from the propulsor to the nuclear reactor in the centre of the submarine is mine. We've got an awful lot of real estate out there. And there are lots of different facets: electrics, provision of hydraulics to the masts and periscopes, control services, ship's services, escape and fire-fighting equipment, and the structural integrity of the hull.

Some submarines have a propulsor, which is an advanced piece of propulsion technology, slightly different to a propeller, in that it's lighter and more efficient, with many more blades than a warship propeller. With fewer blades you get higher cavitations, which are areas of low pressure where air bubbles collapse in the water, creating a 'popping' noise, so the higher the number of blades, the quieter we are in the water, which is obviously desirable for a submarine.

The reactor powers pretty much everything on the boat. It powers the main engines and the turbo generators, which produce electricity for us. We also have a main battery, which provides emergency power and diesel generators that can provide support to the battery. So if the reactor decides it needs to shut down for safety, it does something called a reactor-scram, where it shuts itself down. We then lose propulsion and power for a period of time while we work out what the defect is and recover the reactor.

People don't understand nuclear power, so they're nervous of it. But the pressurised water reactor we operate is inherently safe. It produces steam through the provision of heat to the steam generators. We take the steam, put it through a steam turbine, the steam turbine into a gearbox, gearbox to the shaft, through the shaft train to the propulsor, and that's the provision of main engine power. Nuclear fission reduces as temperature increases – so as the temperature of the primary coolant increases, it naturally wants to reduce the generation of fission. It's what's called load-following and self-regulating.

The risk is from radiation; fission products are the problem. There's gamma radiation, which is caused by the fact we've got nuclear fission on board, then there's the potential of neutrons or gamma-emitters being released from the fuel into the environment, contact with which would damage your DNA. The Russian diplomat who was killed on British soil [ex-KGB officer Alexander Litvinenko], died of acute radiation syndrome after ingesting polonium-210, which is a fission product, and when it's ingested it damages the tissues all the way through the body, leading to organ failure and death, which will be slow or quick, depending on the dose. A leak is very unlikely to occur on our boat because the reactor department is enclosed by a containment boundary, with two airlock doors at either end.

Day to day, work consists of set routines. First thing in the morning, either my deputy or I will brief Command at what's called 'O' group, where all the HODs [heads of department] and relevant people get together and we brief them on any defects we've had overnight. And then there are the set routines, like daily reactor safety checks. We're very focused on maintaining a benign environment for the steam generators, so we look at primary chemistry every one or two days, depending what cycle they're in. Have we got any fission products in the coolant? Are the levels of activation such that we couldn't discharge?

The trouble is that things often go wrong in a submarine. Every trip triggers different challenges because we're managing different defects, concerns and risks. There are the small defects you can manage and there are the big defects where you have to say: 'No, I can't support this operation, I need to come alongside and fix something.'

The last problem we had was to do with hydraulics. We'd been at sea about forty-five minutes when this pump stopped working and then most of the department spent the entire night working on it. These submarines need an awful lot of care and maintenance within a Navy that has budgetary constraints, so it's your responsibility to turn to whoever you've got in your department and use their skills to get the job done.

Boredom sets in when you're on patrol and not much is

happening. You completely lose contact with the outside world. The isolation is total. We've got mail systems, but they don't work when we're maintaining silence, so you can't communicate with your loved ones when you want to.

I've got two children, but I trust my wife totally to bring them up. She keeps me involved and I do play quite an active part in their lives, but she has to make an awful lot of decisions without me. We discussed how it would work before we had children, but I don't think you can fully appreciate the pressures until you have them. It involves a lot of hard work on both sides.

There are a whole load of decisions you usually make as a couple, which my wife will make alone and I just have to trust her to make these decisions on my behalf but also to support her when she does something I don't agree with. You've got to say: 'OK, yeah, happy ...' To be honest, they're usually fairly petty things, like the colour of a sofa, and is it actually worth getting upset about that? Probably not. Fortunately, the majority of important decisions, like nurseries for the children or financial matters, we tend to feel the same way about. A few weeks ago, my wife moved house, so home for me now is Cornwall. I saw the house once, signed all the papers, then left. I don't even remember exactly where it is now. But there we are. If it works out fine, I'm happy.

NICKY ALDER, WIFE OF MARK ALDER

Nicky is married to Mark Alder and has stopped full-time work to look after their two young children.

When we first started going out, Mark was a naval architect working for Lloyd's Register, and a naval reservist, but then he got to a point when he thought, Hang on a minute, there's more to life than this, and he loves the sea, he loves the Navy, so he joined up full time. We had only been together as boyfriend–girlfriend for a couple of months. He's always been very enthusiastic about submarines, although he's never explained why – I've always thought it was because he was short.

I worked as an A&E nurse at the John Radcliffe in Oxford, where I did a week's night shifts and then I'd spend my week off in Portsmouth with Mark, which I soon knew would be part of our lives, because shortly after he moved there, he proposed. He'd booked a holiday on Burgh Island in Devon, and there's a rock that appears at low tide, called Murray's Rock, which is my maiden name, and as Murray's Rock appeared, he popped the question, which I thought was very sweet and romantic.

We were married very shortly after and had two weeks' honeymoon, and then it was, 'Submarines, GO!' I hadn't a clue what being with a submariner would entail, but I soon learned what every naval wife knows, that you're marrying the military first and the man second. That's the way it is and if you don't accept that, you're not going to have a particularly happy time.

The first thing I had to do was move. I had the ideal life in Oxford, a lovely flat, and my perfect job, and I knew then that my career would be taking a massive back seat, but by the time I agreed to marry Mark that was OK by me.

When he went on his first submarine, there was hardly any communication, just an email once in a while.

Although I missed him, while I was working full time and had my lovely work friends, Mark's going off to work didn't really make an impact. It's when children come along that you start to understand what it's all about. In fact, when I was pregnant with Anna, he couldn't make any of my antenatal classes because he just wasn't there, so I would be the single mum on her own, which was horrible, because if you turn up without your partner, they automatically assume you have just decided not to stay with whoever you got pregnant with.

And then I suddenly realised that Mark might not actually make it off the submarine for her delivery, and I was huge and overdue and just feeling absolute rubbish. Fortunately for us, the XO hadn't been able to get off for the birth of his child and he had said, 'No one under my charge is going to miss the birth of their child,' so when he heard Mark's wife was expecting, he pulled every string to make sure he got off, and they flew him off in time – actually, we've got the photos of Mark being winched off the sub by Sea King.

So, Mark came home for the birth – and then went back to work straightaway. And, very sadly, in the first year of her life, Mark didn't see Anna that much.

The fact is that as a wife on your own, you then have to cope with a screaming child. You're called during the night and in the morning, and you don't have any respite. You're the person who gets the child up, puts them to bed and there's nobody to talk to or bounce ideas off.

You can never be quite sure with the Navy of your husband's movements. I never believe what they say about him coming home until it's actually happened. That's not a criticism – it's just a fact that plans change and submarines break down.

It's silly things, like weddings, when I really miss him. Going to weddings on your own with kids is rubbish; it's so much easier having someone there to give you a hand. Also, everyone always asks how Mark is, and then you inevitably get the comments, 'Well, why can't he be here?' or, 'You should put your foot down with the Navy . . . ' I'm fed up explaining that I could put my foot down and have a tantrum, but if he needs to be at sea, he must be there.

The latest issue has been choosing Anna's school. We're so lucky in that we have four primary schools to choose from where we are. I wanted to visit them with Mark. 'Oh no,' he said, 'I haven't got time for that, I'm totally happy with what you choose.' And I think, Well, you need to have time for that, this is your daughter's education . . . But in the grand scheme of things, it's a primary school and I am perfectly able to make that decision myself, and I will choose a very good school and hopefully we'll get accepted.

But I don't know why people choose to be single parents; why would you do that? It's rubbish. Everything is on your own. Last week I had a small car accident, when this lady backed into me. You've got to do the whole process on your own, right from trying to calm down two children who are very shaken up and upset. This lady made Anna miss her ballet class, so we had a three-year-old who couldn't understand why she couldn't do ballet. And then, of course, you're advised to phone your insurance company straightaway, but by the time you get home it's six o'clock, and it's tea, bath, bed and you can't say to a partner, 'Can you just phone the insurance company?' You have to deal with everything.

Like the house move. Mark and I viewed our house, which is lovely, in January. He saw it for about ten minutes and we decided we were going to buy it, and that was it, he left for sea. So I managed the whole lot on my tod, moving everything and everyone lock, stock and barrel, which was absolutely fine, you just have to man-up and get on with it. He phoned me when he came back in May, bless him, saying, 'Where am I going? I don't actually know where it is.'

Oh, it's really exciting when he comes home from a stint away. You can meet the submarine if you want when it comes into Devonport, they have a lovely watching area at the base. It's very moving actually, seeing a submarine come in. It's similar to greeting soldiers back from Afghanistan. OK, they may not have been on the frontline, but they've been away in cramped conditions, they've eaten terrible food, they've got one exercise bike and one rowing machine between the lot of them and they're out of shape and tired. The warfare officers can come off but the engineers have to stay on, so I'll see Mark for about five minutes and then he's got to go back to shut down the reactor. So we now have an understanding that we just wait for him to drive home.

The day before, we'll make a little banner and Anna gets very excited. She'll talk about all the things she's going to do with Daddy. This time, it's going to be Christmas-tree shopping; not a day goes by when she hasn't talked about Christmas-tree shopping with Mark.

It's absolutely fantastic when he does come home; Anna goes ballistic and is climbing the walls with excitement and talking non-stop. I go out of the window when Daddy's home, because Mark is obviously God's gift in Anna's eyes. I'm not allowed to give her a story, I can't feed her, I am bottom of the bottom's bottom, which used to be funny, but is now not so funny. I find it very difficult not to tell him absolutely everything that's happening, and every decision we need to make the minute he comes through the door. I just don't stop talking because I've finally got adult company, and the poor chap gets a bit overwhelmed. So I've learned now to write down everything I need to tell him, and to give it to him in little bits.

He's white as a sheet and a little bit tubby because the diet's terrible, and he's shattered, absolutely shattered. He sleeps badly at first; any loud noise and he's up, although if they've had a good run, it's not so bad. Also, because he hasn't had female company for a while, he's like a flipping limpet and he sort of smothers me, which is lovely, but I haven't had him next to me for weeks and weeks either and I've got used to having a whole bed to myself and spreading out like a starfish, so it just takes us a little while to get used to all that. But it's very, very nice, and we have a forty-eight-hour-window where I just forgive everything.

For instance, he'll say things as if I'm a junior rate.

'You can do that, now!'

'No, actually, you can do it yourself, Mark.'

There are other things, like he'll just drop out of his clothes and walk away. And I'm going, 'Do you think they are going to get to the dirty laundry basket on their own?' What is it with you men, what's difficult about flipping the lid of the laundry basket and putting your things in?

Also, he wants to have a lot of fun with Anna at these times and make sure she remembers him as being a fun, lovely daddy, but also, he needs to discipline her, as I have to, and he's not used to doing that. Well, he does now, that's been one of our big talking points this last year. We've had a very difficult year, with our second child Harry being born and Mark being away, and we've had to properly sit down and talk, and sort out our issues, because if not, he's not going to have a marriage to come home to. Lots of things have come out, but I'm happy to say, we're now stronger than ever.

When he leaves, I feel more desolate than anything, but

I cannot show any of that, because Anna will get upset, so we have to be very bright and jolly.

I'm happy to support Mark in the decision he's made, because if he's happy and his career flies, which it is doing at the minute, then we all benefit, because he doesn't do this all for himself, he does it so we can have a lovely house and a happy family life. But I do have a tiny worry that we will get to our fifties and our children won't be there any more, and we'll sit down and think, Oh God, we've got nothing to talk about because we've spent most of our lives apart. So I keep talking to him, poor chap – he sometimes can't get a word in edgeways. But even if I'm boring him rigid, I think it's very important that he hears what I've got to say and vice versa, so it's all a lovely deposit account, so that when we are fifty, I'll have known all about what's being going on while he's been at sea and he'll have known what's been going on at home.

I have made him promise that when all our children are at university, we can be hippies and go around Australia in a camper van. So we're just going to have our gap year years and years and years late . . .

The camaraderie on board submarine is absolutely fantastic. Because they're a much smaller unit, they're a bit more relaxed at sea than skimmers, so they can grow a beard if the captain allows it – although Mark looks like an idiot in one – and they can use first names under the sea, although not on the surface. Also, the best antenatal classes a man can have are under the sea, because all the boys have children, so their main topic of conversation is their home life. Mark came home for Anna's delivery knowing how to change a nappy, plus he knew loads of remedies for colic and how to make up a bottle, which I thought was absolutely hilarious.

The weekends always seem to stretch out in front of me. By Thursday I'm desperately trying to find activities you can do, because all your friends who have husbands will be doing their own family things and no one wants a single mum with two kids hanging about. So that's why a lot of us naval wives get together. I'm going to spend this weekend with some girls on the married patch. We'll all bring our children and sleep over, get in our pyjamas, have a bottle of wine and watch *Strictly Come Dancing*, and then the next day go for a massive walk and just generally have some adult company. I wouldn't be this sane – if I am – without that group, there's a fantastic camaraderie with military wives, the support network is absolutely fantastic. And when we get together we have a really good bitch about the military. It's fantastic to be able to let off steam to people who understand. We don't need sympathy at all and I don't want to have to explain over and over that it's OK Mark's away; it's the choice I've made. And all of us know, really, in our heart of hearts, that we support our husbands absolutely to the hilt, most of the time.

REAR ADMIRAL MARK ANDERSON

Commander (Operations), Rear Admiral Submarines, Commander Submarines North Atlantic

Rear Admiral Anderson is Fleet Commander Operations, commanding ships, submarines, aircraft and Royal Marines. As Rear Admiral Submarines he describes himself as 'the father figure' of the Submarine Service, and in the Navy he's responsible to the Commander-in-Chief Fleet.

I first went to sea on a diesel submarine called HMS *Finwhale*, and I just loved the professional informality between the officers and other ranks, the sense of fun and shared responsibility; it was like underwater yachting. My first bunk was a torpedo rack in the fore end, so I slept underneath a Mark 8 torpedo, with 960 lbs of Torpex, which is a high-density explosive, dripping diesel fuel on my forehead. And we spent quite a lot of time rolling around on the surface.

I've served on nuclear submarines exclusively since. Being granted command is an incredible privilege, and when I was given command of HMS *Talent*, I was so pleased, it wasn't true. *Talent* was what we called a special-fit submarine. It carried some extra equipment to allow it to do surveillance missions, which meant it had some very special people, and a little bit more of a carefully selected team ... it was absolutely running on sweet oil. We did a number of missions, which I can't talk about – let's just say that's a measure of the importance of some of the things we did – and that talking about it would undoubtedly endanger people, or harm our ability to perform the same sort of operations again.

Three months before I was due to hand over command, I broke my leg, and had to hand over to my XO [executive officer]. You go through what we call 'post-command blues' anyway, and there I was, with a complex fracture, just sat in the garden at home. When you're a commanding officer you're a very important person on your boat, but the day after you're not, and I felt that quite harshly. That probably led to me being pretty miserable and depressed to live with for a while, and certainly contributed to the start of what led to my divorce.

And then I was fortunate enough to be given command of a surface ship, HMS *Marlborough*, a Type 23, which is a general purpose frigate, primarily anti-submarine warfare, so for that command I was a poacher-turned-gamekeeper. The Type 23 has a very long towed array, which is a mile-long cable with a very long linear sonar on the end of it that listens for very low frequency. Low-frequency sound travels a long way in water – which is how whales manage to keep their family groups in contact with each other across oceans.

Currently I'm the Fleet Commander Operations, and as such I exercise operational command of deployed fleet units, ships, submarines, aircraft and Royal Marines once they leave the wall. There's an exception to that, and that's the Gulf and the South Atlantic, so if ships enter there I hand op com over to the operational commander of Permanent Joint Headquarters and keep an overwatch. Another part of my role is as Rear Admiral Submarines, so I'm the tribal chief, the father figure, if you like, of the Submarine Service.

In the Navy I'm known as a head of Fighting Arm, which makes me formally responsible to the First Sea Lord for what's known as the moral component of military capability, the people issues. But because submarines are such a specific skill set, I'm also the subject-matter expert for the commander-in-chief, so people defer to me on the management of submarines.

There are about three hundred submarines worldwide. There are diminishing numbers of submarines in some of the traditional operating areas, but burgeoning submarine operators in new areas, like the Middle East and Singapore; Malaysia and Iran are building small conventional submarines, as are a number of people around the Far East. The Chinese are building nuclear submarines faster than the Americans.

These are people who have learned that well-operated, conventional submarines are terribly difficult to counter, so are a very good means of denying use of the sea to stronger navies that might oppose them. Also, it's very difficult to find and attack a submerged submarine; there are very few countries who can prosecute nuclear submarines successfully.

The thing that submarines do better than anything else is sea denial: they have the ability to stop another country operating surface ships on that sea with impunity. The most obvious example for us was operating submarines around the Falkland Islands before the task group got there. As soon as the *Belgrano* was sunk, the sea supply of the Falklands Islands stopped because they couldn't run the risk of something happening again. In our current strategic position, that's not something we would expect to do.

We have four ballistic missile submarines, the Vanguard class, operating out of Faslane. *Astute* is based in Faslane, and she'll be joined by *Ambush* in a year, and we have five Trafalgar-class subs, including HMS *Torbay*.

We do covert insertion of land forces, and we can do it early-entry; we do intelligence gathering, again, because we're covert. And as you start to deploy and build up force, we're the forward eyes and ears of the task group commander, and the first barrier of defence for that task group or landing force as it comes forward by sea, bearing in mind 80 to 90 per cent of military capacity goes by sea. And of course, we've also got the Tomahawk land-attack missiles, which gives us the ability to attack very specific high-interest targets.

A dived submarine is operating in the best cover available on the military battlefield – the Army would die for the ability to disappear in the way we do, and science has yet to find a failsafe means of finding a dived nuclear submarine. So the relevance of the submarine today is as important as it ever was. They can take a measure of what another hostile country is doing without distorting their activity, which you would if you flew an aircraft over the top – people would stop practising whatever they were doing. But if you go in with a submarine and loiter, they'll carry on doing what they're preparing to do. It's what we call indications and warnings. What are the enemy up to? How have they changed their posture? Are they using more specific war-fighting capabilities than they would normally expose in training? And we can detect these sorts of things and report back.

While dived, we're trying to use enduring stealth. We make no transmissions; in fact, the commanding officer has to personally approve every single transmission, from ditching gash – slinging rubbish out of the boat – to transmitting on the radio. Eventually, though, we need to put a mast above the water that can detect radars, visually confirm targets and bring in the broader intelligence picture, and build and download that picture photographically so we can see it. That is the moment of vulnerability.

A very great specific of submarines is that they tend to operate as independent platforms. I will put them into an area, give them a job to do and let them get on with it, and I only hear how well they've done their job when they break radio silence. By doing that, I give them the maximum opportunity to stay hidden: they don't have to come to periscope depth to hear from me, although they have to take a certain amount of traffic, for instance, if the water they were allocated changes because another submarine's coming through, I have to tell them that for their safety. We do a traffic control function at Northwood through the Submarine Movement Advisory Authority, which is run from Commander Task Force 311 on behalf of NATO.

My headquarters, Commander Task Force 345, is responsible for keeping a submarine at sea on continuous at sea deterrents, within the required notice to fire, which is the length of time they have to release their missiles in accordance with a lawful order from the Prime Minister. These lengths of time depend on the level of threat. We have reduced from the 'as soon as you possibly could do it' time scale that existed at the end of the Cold War to something that is more appropriate to the current state measured in days.

One of my jobs is to make sure that the nuclear deterrent can operate without it being detected by anybody, including friendly forces, as has happened throughout the past four decades we've been operating it so far.

The Prime Minister is responsible for making the decision about the release of nuclear weapons. He generates within the Cabinet Office, or an alternative headquarters if he needs to be in one, a legal and accountable national firing message, which comes to my headquarters and is translated promptly into a coded firing message for the submarine. That firing message is received and validated on board the submarine in a way that the submarine cannot interpret in terms of the target, and they instruct the system to respond to that preordained target set, and fire off a number of missiles at the Prime Minister's direct command.

There are means by which a commanding officer receives instructions as to what he is to do, should the fabric fall. The Prime Minister will write a letter, popularly known as the 'letter of last resort', although we know it as something else, which he signs, and it will be delivered personally to every CO who could be deployed. Each CO puts it in his safe, and it is only opened *in extremis*. And we're in a fairly appalling position if he's opening that letter . . .

CHIEF PETTY OFFICER (SONAR) RICHIE BARROW

A senior sonar rating, CPO Barrow is responsible for the operation of the sonar system. He can recognise and classify the signatures of all ships and submarines to inform tactical decisions.

The Atlantic, the Mediterranean, the Pacific are all very much the same, but the Arctic is my favourite ocean. You get up to the Arctic, and it's completely different. Where ice is starting to form, you get ambient sound all around the submarine, cracking and groaning, and as you get further and further inside the marginal ice zone, you get larger blocks of ice, which literally creak and groan and crunch and smash against each other. Then, all of a sudden, as soon as you get to the ice cap, it goes completely quiet.

Amazingly quiet. Quieter than anywhere else on the planet.

There is lots of bio in that area, too. One of the boys will say: 'I've got whales over here . . .' and everyone will want to gather round and listen to them. It really gets to the guys. I'll be honest with you, when you're stuck on board, a million miles away from your family, the whales will make a grown man cry. It's a noise that gets hold of you straight away, they sound so sad and lost, you feel sorry for them. It's almost like sound a baby would make. You want to say, 'Come over here and let me give you a cuddle, it's OK, you're not on your own.' They just capture your heart and your imagination. The other sounds I love to hear are the porpoises – they make lots of little clicking and squeaking noises. We've got cameras fixed to the submarine, so you can actually see them swimming round the boat. Whales are so large you can sometimes mistake them for submarine contacts, because the flow noise over their smooth bodies creates the same sound in the water.

But the sound I want to hear most of all is: 'Fall out from harbour stations below,' because it means we're alongside the wall. And that means I'm going home. I've been married ten years and I've got a two-year-old daughter, and certainly the most difficult part is that first day at sea, away from home, having left our loved ones. But the strange thing is when you return, thirty, sixty, ninety days later, it's as if time stood still at home. Also, you come off, and you're amazed how quiet everything is without the ventilation pounding in your ears.

Basically, I've been in uniform since I was six. I was in the Cubs, followed by the Scouts and Sea Cadets. I thought I was joining the Navy to go on ships, but once I'd done my basic training, I was streamed: 'Barrow,' they said, 'you're going on submarines,' and I went into the Submarine Service aged sixteen, which was a complete shock to me. But I certainly wouldn't want to change now.

There's more of a close-knit community on a submarine, everyone has to rely on everyone else, whereas with the greater numbers on a ship, you're just a number. Also, on a ship, you're in charge of a department, and here you're aware of everything that's going on. I'm expected to know all the hydraulic valves and the valves back aft in the engine room, as much as the engineers back aft have to know about my sonar.

My role is to manage a team of thirteen crew members; we man sonar dive twenty-four-seven, tracking and classifying surface and sub-surface units, and provide Command with classification, be they warships, submarines or fishing vessels. As soon as we dive, we become the eyes and ears of the submarine.

Sonar stands for sounds, navigation and ranging, and there are three types: passive, active and narrow band.

Passive – or listening – is done through barrier, flank and fin sonar arrays situated all along the front and sides of the submarine; it's a bit like having a hydrophone in the water which feeds into thousands of processors. The more you've got, the better the range and the better the bearing accuracy.

Active sonar is us transmitting a pulse via active projectors – a return echo then comes back from a reflective surface, like a ship or another submarine, giving us bearing and range. We've got sonars on board capable of looking for tethered mines and high-definition sonars we can use when we're looking underneath a ship, or to check the thickness of surface ice. But, once we transmit an active sonar, we go from covert to overt nature, which means we've given our position away.

Narrow band breaks the whole broadband symphony of sound into its individual parts. I can identify a warship with my bow passive sonar, but what Command needs to know is what kind of warship it is. So we can say, 'It's got two shafts and five blades,' and only a number of warships have that configuration. But that wouldn't be enough to justify firing a weapon at it, so we then use narrow bands to look at the different frequencies of sound transmitted through the hull, which tells us about all the rotating machinery on board. Then we'll get out our reference books and be able to say: 'That was a Type 23 frigate' or 'That's HMS

Westminster.' My newest sound is HMS *Astute*. We were listening to her on the surface and immediately started recording and analysing her; so now, if we ever come across her again, we've got the reference material.

My role is to tell the captain the submarine's optimal search and listening depth, which would be at periscope depth of 17½ metres. The best evasion depth is different: if we want to evade a warship we need to be as close to the sea bed as possible. We map out all the waters around the world to create historical data, including where all the wrecks and pinnacles are, and we need to loiter in those positions so the ship's sonar will get lots of reflective echoes going off all over the place.

The average speed of sound in water is 1500 metres per second, but it varies depending on salinity, depth and temperature. In April you get a seasonal thermocline when warmth from the sun starts to heat the surface of the sea, penetrating 30 or 40 metres and giving us a faster speed.

The water column, or isovelocity, changes with the seasons, or rather the top does – we're in a permanent thermocline. But when you go off the continental shelf, about 150 miles off the coast, we're looking at waters in excess of 3000 metres deep and the bottom never changes. The water depth on the continental shelf doesn't generally go beyond 200 metres, so if we were to have an accident, we are within escape limits. But once we leave it, we enter a region of no return. The maximum recorded escape from a submarine is 180 metres. If we go down beyond our deep diving depth or crush depth – the submerged depth at which a submarine's hull will collapse due to pressure – there is no escape.

ABLE SEAMAN (TACTICAL SYSTEMS) SAM BETTS

A picture-compilation operator within the control room, AB Betts also operates the electronic warfare equipment to warn of enemy-threat radars.

I always wanted to join the Navy. I don't know why, because I've got no family that were in the Navy. My mum always says to me, 'What's the fascination with the Navy?' and I can't give her an answer, it's just been in my head since being a toddler.

I wanted to live life a little bit before I joined, so I worked part-time in the home-shopping department of ASDA straight from school, just general dogsbody, really. There wasn't a career in it but, for what it was, it was brilliant, something to pass the time before I started with the Navy.

I joined the boat in Dubai, which was exciting; I went straight from SMQ, which is where you learn to be a sub-mariner, and flew to Dubai. I'd never been to the Middle East before and since then I've been to the Middle East three or four times, as this boat has done a lot of east of Suez running.

It's very hot out there and they have a different life and culture, which you have to respect, but to be honest, there's not a whole lot to do, unless you go into the actual city of Dubai, which is amazing. Unfortunately, we were staying in Fujairah, which is at least two hours away from Dubai. The second time we went there was the best, because we had a ship's company barbecue. We all went to the senior rates' hotel and they had an amazing barbecue laid on and drinks, plus all these water sports: banana boats and jet skis, all paid for by the fund on board.

On my third visit, we went to Souda Bay which is known as a party town, and a really good place to be if you have done a long trip; it came after a long running period, we had done three months at sea without surfacing. So you can imagine coming alongside and seeing the bay – well, everyone wants to unwind and have a good laugh with the boys.

The bars there are pretty similar to normal bars in England, except the majority of them are run by Eastern Europeans. On the last day before we sailed, one of the bar owners said, 'Right, you have spent a lot of money in my bar, come down on Sunday morning.' And he had laid on a massive spread of food, with all this free drink, which was his way of saying, 'Thank you for putting money into my business' – which you would never get in England.

The best part of this job is the people you meet, the places you go. The bad parts are that it is very awkward having a relationship when you work on submarines, especially this one, with all the running we do, we are away such a lot. Don't get me wrong, if someone comes along, great. But I don't have anyone right now. Fortunately, I am only twenty years old, so there's a lot of time for that later on.

Another bad thing, and something you don't hear about too much when you are joining, are duties, particularly the duties when we come alongside. You spend the whole time aboard the submarine and you have to go up and do end trots, the casing has to be manned twenty-four-seven with the gun trot. And that is purely and simply standing there with an SA80, while the QM (quartermaster) checks IDs to make sure everyone who is supposed to get on can get on, and those who shouldn't can't.

I've enjoyed being in TS (tactical systems) and I like the lads there, but ultimately it doesn't appeal to me. I would like to work back aft as a marine engineer. One of the boys I joined up with is an ME and he just loves it; every time

I come off watch, I'm looking forward to getting into my bed because I've just had enough of it, but he's coming off watch, and he's like, 'I can't wait to go back on watch.' That's how I want to be, I don't want to get too annoyed with everything and end up leaving. So I am branch transferring, and hopefully going to become a marine engineer. I've been back there and talked to the other MEs, and they're all keen and think it's a good idea.

Also, you get nuclear qualifications on board submarines as an ME and if you are good at it there might be jobs outside, hopefully. The job I do now, well, there's not a lot outside the Navy like it, so it's sort of thinking ahead a little bit.

This job has matured me a lot. It's probably because I have much more responsibility than when I was a civvy and working in ASDA; just the fact that within four or five weeks after you join the Navy, you have a rifle in your hand, and you are shooting. Within a year you are on your first seagoing submarine and within eighteen months doing patrols – and then you really are doing a grown-up's job.

Two years after I joined, I look back at things and think what a kid I was before I joined the Navy. And what am I like now? Well, you can't be a kid because if something happens, you have to react to it appropriately, do the right thing and stop it, because if something goes wrong these are such confined spaces that we could be in mortal danger, so it needs a real grown-up to be there.

But don't get me wrong, you can still have a laugh, and that's what keeps me in the job. The fun you have sitting in the junior rates' mess is amazing – all the boys are quality.

PETTY OFFICER (MEDICAL ASSISTANT) BENJAMIN COWLEY

PO Cowley is the medical branch senior rating responsible for the diagnosis and treatment of any of ship's company should they fall ill. He's also responsible to Command for the radiological protection measures required to operate the nuclear reactor.

Everyone calls me 'Doc' and I'm regarded as a senior medical officer, although I'm not a real medical officer, it's just an honorary title. I also deal with the reactor and radiation protection, which is the main job.

I've had eighteen months medical training and taken various courses around the country. I guess I'm equivalent to a paramedic, with additional skills – prescribing and resetting broken bones and a bit of nursing is involved as

87

well, because if we have a casualty, we have to look after him from start to finish. If we need to put someone on bed rest, we do all the bed baths and toilets in the bed. Anyone who is injured goes into my bunk, which is not particularly spacious, but it's got more head room than the normal beds; you can actually sit up in it, and there's the ability to curtain it off from the rest of the bunks. But access to the bunk space is very small, so if I need to put someone onto a stretcher, they have got to go somewhere else, the XO's bunk more than likely, although that is very tight too.

Because of the lack of space on a submarine, my stores are dotted all over the place, so even if I need something in a hurry I have to go searching. Dry dressings are down on three deck, all the spare fluids are in the senior rates mess, my spare oxygen is aft, in the engine room, and my control cabinet for drugs is kept in the captain's office safe.

Originally I wanted to be a nurse, but my granddad and uncle were in the Navy, and I've always been into sailing and quite like being at sea. Anyway, I joined the Navy from Sea Cadets. My class got streamed for either Royal Marines or Submarine Service, and I got the Submarines – although I actually would have preferred the Royal Marines, so I wasn't exactly happy about that. I was a little apprehensive the first time I got on a submarine, as I was used to being on ships where you can go out on the upper deck and see a bit of sunlight, and not being locked away. But it wasn't majorly intimidating.

I think we submariners tend to look on life a bit differently to most people because we work in an inherently dangerous environment, so you are taking your life in your hands every day. Everyone seems to have a warped sense of humour, you get some very sick jokes coming out. Also, you can't have your own personal space, so nothing's private, and if you make a mistake in your work, everyone knows about it.

Frankly, it's not a really healthy environment. The air we breathe is full of oil and dust particles churned around, and there are high levels of carbon monoxide. Viruses spread like wildfire on a submarine because it is a closed atmosphere and the atmosphere is recirculated all the time, which is why we tend to get coughs and colds in the first two weeks at sea, and the last few weeks when people are run down.

A few days ago we had two cases of diarrhoea and vomiting, which we managed to clear up, but another two have just appeared. It's a potentially serious situation, because if everyone were to get it, we wouldn't be able to function. So I now have to notify Fleet we have a problem on board – two and above you have to tell the Fleet – and if the problem continues, they will send a team down to investigate whether someone brought it on board with them or whether the problem emanates from on board, and they'll speak to people and trace back what they've eaten and where they've been to eat.

Everyone we now find with D&V is getting twenty-four hours off work and clear fluids, clear tea, clear coffee or water, nothing with any sugar in it, just to clear the system out. Also, everyone is reminded to wash their hands after going to the toilet, and we're taking away the communal towels and increasing the cleaning of the heads, which are now being cleaned every hour.

Other than the D&V, we have nothing out of the ordinary at the moment, a few coughs and colds, and a few cuts and grazes. People bang their heads all the time on a sub, although they don't come and see us about that. Because I'm six foot three inches, I do it every day, and usually at exactly the same spot, going into the senior rates room.

The captain's in charge of circulation of air, but I advise on what levels we need to keep it at. There are eight different readings and we monitor the air every four hours. We play about with the oxygen levels; we top out quite high and we change the ampage on the electrolysers to produce more or less oxygen depending on how far up the band we are, and we add hydrogen to the primary circuit to scavenge for oxygen. The basic kit we need are electrolysers, which produce oxygen, scrubbers, which take out carbon dioxide, and carbon monoxide burners that get rid of carbon monoxide, plus we have different types of filters all over the place.

I'm just getting this draft done, another eighteen months to go, and then three years on board, and that's my twenty-two years done. I was thinking of maybe becoming a train driver or a bus driver; there's a train station near where my wife and I live and it would then be incredibly easy to go to work.

ENGINEERING TECHNICIAN (WEAPONS ENGINEER) STEVEN CRESSWELL

A member of the Bomb Shop team, AB Cresswell is involved in the maintenance of the heavyweight torpedos and cruise missiles on board. He also watch-keeps in the control room, operating ship's systems such as ventilation, masts and periscopes.

I worked as an estate agent for years; I started at the beginning of the five-year boom, when all the prices were shooting up, and I sold a couple of houses for over a million pounds – I sold one plot to a builder who built several houses on it, and we sold each of those for a million. So they were good times. But there were rumblings the market was going bad and suddenly the Halifax withdrew their 100 per cent mortgages out of the blue. Also, things started getting a bit messy and back-bitey at the company I worked for and people began being forced out left, right and centre. I saw what was happening to other people and I jumped rather than be pushed, and began looking for alternative employment. I was thirty-two.

All the other jobs I went for were, 'No, ta, we don't want old people like you.' I considered going into the Armed Forces, although I worried I might be too old, so I went down to the careers office in Nottingham and asked them if I could apply for the Services. They said they'd actually welcome me with open arms.

Originally I didn't know which service to go for. But I soon realised it would have to be the Navy, as I have a huge love for the sea and have had my own boat for years. I didn't intend to go for being a submariner at first, but the more I looked into it, the more it appealed. Also, I met a few submariners, and they were different to the rest of the Navy lads, they were more welcoming, more enthusiastic. Also, they knew their stuff. If you speak to normal sailors, they know about their branch, but nobody else's; say you were talking to a weapons engineer and asked him something about mechanical engineering, they wouldn't know anything about it. But you could ask submariners about anything on board a submarine and they would know the answers straight away. And that professionalism appealed, and I thought, If I'm going to do this amount of learning at my time of life, I'm going to make it as hard as possible for myself.

So I found a position with the Submarine Service and they made me feel really worthwhile. That was great because my pride had taken a bit of a battering; I couldn't afford to live in my house any more, and had gone from living in the second most expensive village in Nottinghamshire to living with my sister in an old council house, plus I'd lost my car and split up with my wife. So I'd taken a bit of a tumble, and I saw joining the Royal Navy and wearing the uniform as an opportunity to get a bit of my pride and dignity back, working towards something useful and worthwhile.

During basic training I got a lot of stick; I was literally twice as old as some of the lads, and I was given the nickname 'Dad' – and that was one of the politer ones.

But there were some advantages to being that age. I had spent years ironing and washing shirts, doing all those domestic things, so that wasn't a problem for me, whereas for some of the lads it was the first time they had even turned on an iron. Plus, I had done a fair bit of camping and outdoor activities, so Dartmoor was never going to be too scary, nor was knocking around in the cold sea, as I'd had my own boat out when it was freezing, whereas the lads hated the cold water and panicked. Also, I could see through a lot of the games the instructors played: I knew when it was the time of the week to get a bollocking – no matter how well you had done, they were going to knock you down to build you back up again. A lot of the lads got quite upset by it, but I could see it for the game it was.

I hadn't done any physical exercise for several years, but I got myself pretty fit before I joined up, and practised my mile and a half, which is what they judge you on, and got my time down to ten and a half minutes, which is the time to pass if you are under eighteen. So I was quite happy with that.

Also, I joined at thirty-two as a smoker and drinker, but there was a 'no alcohol' rule for the first nine weeks of basic training. The weight just fell off me and I actually felt and looked a lot better. I had two weeks' leave over Christmas and my girlfriend didn't recognise me when I got off the train.

But I was a grumpy, insular person during that holiday, because my mindset was still in the basic training; to be perfectly honest, I just wanted to go back and get it done. But once phase one was finished, we had a big passing-out parade and I was right at the front chucking my cap in the air, and I could feel myself change from being totally stressed to being totally relieved, and I made it up with my girlfriend, who's actually been very supportive. Going away to sea was very sudden, but she never grumbles, and just lets me get on with it; she would rather I do something like this with my life than not really do anything, plus there's nothing out there for me in civvy street.

So things are all right, really, with the girlfriend. I can't regularly email her at sea, but I think it would be difficult to be in contact all the time, it would make it worse. This way, you know where you are after your goodbyes, and I think it's best to get on with it, because it would drag you down otherwise.

I only joined the boat in January, so I am still going through the BSQ, the Basic Submarine Qualifications. I have done my forward walk-rounds, where we have to identify the valves and the isolating systems, and prove we know them to a member of staff, and get it signed off. I have got my oral board on Monday, which is my final big interview, and once I've done that I'll get my dolphins, and that will be the end of a very long two years' training. Basically, it's the final check to make sure you do know and understand everything on board, rather than just blagging it. The questions I struggle with are the ones regarding the harbour watches, where you have to go through each crew member and who they are, the DEO and the TASO, and what position they do on that particular watch. At the moment it's just a list of names and numbers and letters, and I struggle remembering all of them. I will have to learn them all parrot-fashion, just to get through it.

The famous dolphins ceremony when you pass your exams happens up on the deck with the captain. He gives you half a glass of rum, at the bottom of which are your dolphins, and after you drain it, you catch it in your teeth. It's an old tradition.

Because I was last to join the boat, at this moment I'm general dogsbody; if anything needs cleaning, fetching, or getting, it's my job. As well as that, I'm moving weapons from the Bomb Shop: the tubes for the Tomahawk missiles are in need of washing every thirty days, so yesterday we took all those out, and we have to put them all back in again today. There are many other items of equipment around the boat we have to maintain too, raising and lowering the periscopes in the control room, plus we have jobs around the boat, like cleaning the sanitary tanks and brushing the heads – and an even worse job is getting rid of sewage out of the tank.

At first a lot of my friends and family thought I was mad when I joined the Sub Service and I got a lot of stick. But my mum's been really great about it – I think she has known for some time I needed something like this in my life – and my girlfriend thinks it's great. Also, my family all make it very easy for me by taking care of things that need to be dealt with when I'm away from home, like banking and that sort of thing. So everyone has been very supportive and tell me they are very proud of me, which feels great.

CAPTAIN MIKE DAVIS-MARKS OBE

Capt Davis-Marks is a former commanding officer of a T-class submarine. He is currently Director of Naval Recruiting for the Royal Navy.

I can't really explain this, there being no obvious catalyst or influence that generated this life-changing decision. I don't remember watching a naval war film on television the night before, I don't live near a naval port, and my father isn't ex-Navy, but I simply woke up one morning when I was about seven or eight and declared to my surprised parents that I wanted to join the Navy. And that decision shaped the rest of my life. I joined the Sea Scouts, rather than the Scouts, I took to boating and sailing, and rowing and yachting, and I applied to join the Royal Navy at the very earliest opportunity, which, for me, was fifteen. And that's all I've ever wanted to do, and I still enjoy doing it now, so it can't have been the wrong decision.

My first experience of submarines at Dartmouth was thoroughly unpleasant and almost ruled them out as an option. It was an old and smelly Oberon-class, diesel-electric submarine, which spent too much time rolling about on the surface in rough weather and making everyone on board sick.

But at that time, the bit of the Navy that was most engaged with operations was the Submarine Service; they were on the frontline, chasing Soviet submarines around the ocean and doing all sort of derring-do things, and the surface Navy was not in the same league, frankly.

Also, I fell in love with the new breed of Trafalgar-class submarines and loved every minute on them. A submarine's progress is very smooth; it feels a bit like flying in a jumbo jet at very low speed, except with no turbulence. In fact, she's not that dissimilar to an aircraft: because of her shape she banks like an aircraft, so if you can imagine a 747 when it turns to starboard, one wing goes down and one wing goes up, a submarine does the same. When a submarine goes through the water it has four fins, called planes – two at the bow, the fore-planes, and two at the stern, the aft-planes – which come out sideways and change the angle and depth of the submarine, and you have someone pulling back and forth on what looks like an aircraft joystick, controlling the planes.

Everyone needs to understand everyone else's job on a submarine. So a young submariner's first three months in a submarine is spent in a pair of overalls crawling around the bilges; he'll have to trace all the systems – the ballast system, the electrical system, hydraulic systems, the air systems – and get to know every component of them, so if there's an emergency, no matter what it is, and you're the person nearest to it, you can deal with it because you understand it. The bottom line is that you don't have the time to save a submarine that you would with a surface ship. For instance, if you have a fire on a ship, it's still going to float; a fire in a submarine is fatal within seconds. You have to stop a flood within seconds otherwise you will be in a very dangerous situation; you have to stop a hydraulic leak instantly, because it might create a fire. And so you need to rely on the people who are on the scene when something happens; they need to deal with it immediately, and we give everybody the same basic level of technical knowledge, which allows them to respond to an emergency if they are the person on the scene.

You want to ensure that the people running your nuclear deterrents are of the highest calibre, and Perisher, which is the submarine commanding officers' course, is one of the toughest courses in the military. It has a reputation as one of the most challenging courses you could put anyone through, mentally and physically. And certainly, that's what

Perisher is there to do. At the end of the day you want someone who commands a nuclear submarine – which is what this course qualifies you to do – to be the best, you don't want a numpty doing it.

Perisher is also about learning to cope with failure of the systems, and relying on yourself. Perisher tests your decision-making, physically and mentally. The commanding officer of the course is known as Teacher, and Teacher will push you to the very limit of your abilities.

For example, in some exercises, you must assume that everything that can help you stops helping you: your computer systems go down, and Teacher wants to see if you can continue an attack without any computer aid; he wants to see that you can look through a periscope and size up what's going on, keep the submarine safe and press home the attack without computers telling you where you are and what you are doing.

You'll be dived in an area of water at periscope depth, and there will be a number of ships buzzing round and they will have been told by Teacher, who's in communication with them, where the sub is and told to charge the submarine if they see it. So you've got to work out if you should go deep, and your aim is to try and get a torpedo into the high-value unit, and they'll charge you, and you've got to deal with that, and do it all without computers, because they've switched them off. You're trying to work out, how far is that? We'll use split-rangefinders, which are mechanical and not electrical, and you have to work out in your head what the range is: if he turned towards me and charged, how quickly would he be on top of me? How quickly do I need to be at safe depth to avoid getting hit? Meanwhile, a stoker will wander into the control room with a broken arm, and the Steward who's planing will suddenly have a heart attack, and your computers have fallen away, and the navigator will say, 'I don't think we are where we are!' And you've not felt pressure like that before, but you've got to deal with it and you either cope with it or you don't. On Perisher they test the extremes because they want to know that you can cope. You learn your strengths and weaknesses, and where your capabilities are in extreme conditions.

You can fail at any time. I was on a course of six people, and two failed; one failed a week from the end, and the other failed a day from the end. If Teacher reaches the point where he decides you are not going to make it, there's not enough improvement to reach the standard by the end of the course, he will arrange for a helicopter or boat to come in then and there, and fifteen minutes before it's due to arrive, he will summon the unlucky student to his cabin, while at the same time his fellow students are packing his bags. 'I'm very sorry to tell you, but you've failed,' he'll say, and he will give a tot of whisky to the guy, and they'll talk about why he failed, because it's a life-changing moment.

And at the end of that fifteen minutes, his kit's brought up, the submarine surfaces, opens hatches, and the guy will be led up by Teacher and put on board the helicopter or boat, whichever way Teacher has got him off, and he's heading back to shore. And from that point on, having failed Perisher, he will never serve in a submarine at sea again.

A few years later, I became captain of my first submarine. When we're preparing for the off, an hour before we sail, my four heads of departments will line up outside my cabin door. You have four heads of department in a submarine: you have a marine engineer, a weapons engineer, a logistics officer and the executive officer, known as XO, your second-in-command.

You want to know from your marine engineer that the engines and all engineering systems are ready to proceed; from your weapons engineer that all your radar, sonar, periscopes and electrical systems are ready, and from logistics that you are stored for sea, and you have to ask silly things like, 'Have we got enough loo paper on board?' And then your second-in-command will confirm he's content that all the right number of people are on board, the right preparations have been made, everything is ready and tested, and that the submarine is ready to proceed.

At that point you turn to your second-in-command and say, 'Very good, pipe harbour stations,' which is the executive order to get everyone in the right place to leave harbour, and to let them know we're about to go to sea, and there's about an hour's worth of getting everything ready to go, ropes need to be unfurled, gangways need to be taken off, flags need to be changed round, people need to get into the right position and ready for the off.

In fact, every order or instruction will be repeated back to check the recipient has received and understood it. For example, if I say 'Pipe the submarine to harbour stations,' XO will say, 'Pipe the submarine to harbour stations, aye aye, sir,' and that tells me he has heard my order correctly and understood it, and he's going to go and do it. Everything in a submarine is repeated back because it's absolutely fundamental we don't have a situation, which apparently occurred during the First World War, when the urgent telegram 'Send reinforcements, we're going to advance' turned into 'Send three and fourpence, we're going to a dance', with dire consequences …

When, finally, your second-in-command confirms that the entire submarine is ready, he will say, 'The submarine is in all respects ready to go to sea, sir.'

And at that point you will go ashore and see your shore captain, called Captain SM, SM being short for submarines, because all the submarines have a shore infrastructure which supports them. You report to him, 'I'm about to take my submarine to sea, sir. All's well,' and salute him, and he'll wander back down the jetty with you. You then climb on board and go straight up to the bridge, at which point the navigator will say, 'All systems have been checked, sir,' and he'll tell you what state the propulsion and the main engines are in, what the reactor's doing, and you repeat it all.

Most orders today are not given by pipes, as we have a Tannoy, but we still use the terminology. A century ago, or more, because of the noise of the wind in the sails and riggings, all the orders were done by whistles or pipe (and an order given by whistle is called a pipe), and there would be all sorts of complex whistle sounds. In fact, some pipes are still used today. 'Pipe the sides' is a long, still, one-note, where everyone stands to attention and salutes, because it means 'Admiral X is coming on board'. 'Pipe the carry on' is a two-tone, which means he's now gone, you can relax.

After my report from the navigator, I will then say, 'Roger, I have the ship.' That is the only time you use the word ship for our boat. It's an expression used in boats and subs alike, and we don't change it because we're in a boat. That means I have taken charge of the boat and everyone's now focused on me.

I will instruct the XO to control the tugs that pull the submarine out; normally there are two tugs tied on because a submarine is very difficult to manoeuvre on the surface in tight waters. When the submarine is free from any hazards and pointing in the right direction, I'll tell the number one to let go of the tugs, and as the seconds count up to the hour we've agreed we're going to sail, I tell him to let go of the ropes.

I'll then get the report, 'All ropes gone,' and I'll give a propulsion order: 'Slow ahead, main engines,' which is the order to turn the propulser, and we'll then start propelling on the surface under our own steam, down the narrow channel out of Devonport, which used to be our home port, with tugs standing by to assist if need be.

We proceed down the Hamoaze, which is the river that leads out to Plymouth Sound, and it winds its way around all sorts of points, coming quite close to land in a couple of areas, one of which is called Devil's Point. A lot of families who didn't make it to the jetty will have gone to stand on Devil's Point, and there are big banners, saying, 'Good luck, HMS *Turbulent*,' and they'll be cheering, and there might be a band playing somewhere as well. It's quite an emotional thing.

And then suddenly it's the open sea and you have got to go back to the reality of getting the submarine ready to get under water.

At the point you're ready to go, you say, 'Pipe the submarine to diving stations.' And when it's reported back that everything's ready – 'Submarine is in all respects ready to dive, sir' – you take a last look at everything in the control room. The control room is the main nerve centre; it's not only where the battles are fought from and where the periscopes are, it's also where the submarine is driven from. And when you've made sure you're happy with the submarine, it's, 'Dive the submarine,' and a pipe's made as the submarine's about to dive: 'Diving now, diving now.' The reason we make that pipe is to alert people we're about to go under water, and that there will be at an angle on the boat, so to make sure their stowage is correct. If you're going to be changing depth and rolling around and going up and down, you don't want to have loose gear lying around, because it could fly off and hurt someone, particularly if it's heavy, and also you don't want to create noise that someone – the enemy – might hear, so there's a lot of emphasis on making sure things are stowed properly in secure lockers that can't be opened. 'Stowed for sea' is the expression.

You can soon hear all the things falling off when you've got 10 or 15 degrees of angle on the submarine.

Once you dive the submarine, the first thing you need to do is get the air out of the ballast tanks, so you do what we call 'rock the bubble,' which means you create a down angle and then an up angle, you shut the vents, because they're still open at this point, and you carry out post-diving checks, and their aim is to make sure that now you're under water there's no water coming in and also to make sure all the systems are working properly. And that's it; the submarine stays submerged until such time you need to surface.

The ocean depth is a complex environment to operate in, it's got many characteristics, and the more a submariner understands those characteristics, the better he can exploit them. For instance, the ocean has different salinities and your buoyancy changes according to the salinity of water, so salty water, like the Mediterranean, is much more difficult to navigate in than where it's uniformly all the same.

Some areas of the ocean and the seas move very fast, particularly when they're channelled through a tight space, so you can be pushed at very high speeds. Around the isle of Guernsey for example, you can get 6–12 knots, and off the western coast of Scotland there's a gulf that goes up to 40 knots. Generally the currents in the oceans are very much slower, of the order of half a knot, or 1 knot, but the closer you get to land, the effect of current becomes greater, and there are also changes according to the wind strengths – a strong wind will generate a current of its own.

The oceans not only move, but they move in different directions at different levels, because you have this convection current. So you've got water masses going in different depths, according to the temperature: a cold slug of water from the Antarctic will be moving south, while warm water generated near the Equator or the tropical zones is moving north above it. In the Second World War, submarines used to move into and out of the Straits of Gibraltar using different layers of water. So submarines who wanted to creep into the Straits of Gibraltar would come in deep, carried by the cold Atlantic water going into the Med, and would go out through the surface slug.

Another way in which we exploit water is that sound waves travel through water, but not in a straight line – they tend to bend, according to either temperature or salinity or depth – and that means you create shadow zones, zones where sound waves don't penetrate, because of the different layers of water. A submarine which has knowledge of those layers would exploit that by hiding in the shadow zones, so it can't be heard. It's all a game of cat and mouse.

A Trafalgar-class submarine has about a hundred bunks, but commonly we will take more people than that to sea, because we have a training requirement, so you might find as many as 120, 150 people on board. So that means many will be sharing bunks. Someone who is on watch will have an opposite number who's off watch asleep in the bunk, and then when they change over, the bunk is still warm from the previous incumbent – which is why we call it hot-bunking. But we do not share bedding; everyone has their own bedding.

Food is immensely important in a submarine, it's one of the things that binds the crew together. We have giant fridges and freezers on board, which store up to three months' worth of food, and you need to carry a lot for 120-plus people for three months. The ability of the chefs to create mouth-watering recipes from the dry and frozen provision stores is amazing. Fresh bread is baked every day from raw ingredients and if you're on the early morning watch, there's nothing nicer than the smell of baking bread drifting up from the galley; it makes you want the watch to end quickly so you can sit down to breakfast. We carry a small amount of fresh food, but it's of limited supply and runs out after a time, so most of our food is either dry or frozen. Pizzas are made by hand, steak and kidney pie has pastry made by hand, with tins of steak and kidney poured in.

We watch DVDs most nights, and quiz nights are one night a week. Occasionally, we dress up and 'Go to the races'. We tie a wooden horse on a track that's laid out in a submarine passageway, and there's money put on it, usually going to charities. There is a small library on board, which is replenished each trip. Also, some people are doing further education, so there will be correspondence courses, and some people have hobbies; somebody recently built a matchstick replica of HMS *Victory*, although I prefer to look at the real thing.

You can do things in a submarine that you just can't do in any other vessel. Once, for example, we were operating in the Arctic Ocean with two American submarines, doing tactical development, learning how to operate against each other under the ice cap in case we had to fight the Russians there. So we were playing cat and mouse, trying different positions and set-ups.

Operating under the ice cap is an extraordinary feeling, there's a sense of excitement and adventure that you're doing something rather unique and special. But there's an element of risk, being under the Pole, so you have to ensure that the inertial navigation system is sufficiently 'groomed', which means it's not getting errors, because you don't want to get lost under the ice cap.

Also, our submarines are strengthened to allow them to routinely surface through one metre of ice, and three metres in an emergency, but there are lots of bits of the Arctic where the ice is much thicker than three metres.

Fortunately, at the end of our manoeuvres, we were all safe, and surfaced our vessels together.

All three submarines were within walking distance of each other, and, leaving a small skeleton crew on board, we got off our submarines, tightly wrapped up in our thermals, and climbed out onto the ice. It was cold, but there wasn't much wind blowing, so the chill factor was quite low. It was stunningly beautiful, with a bright blue sky and no clouds at all, and the sun, rather oddly, went round in a perfect circle high in the sky, and we watched it go around. We played all sorts of games on the ice. First was tug-of-war, and then we played American football, and after that we taught them how to play ice cricket, and then someone erected a red-and-white striped pole marked 'North Pole', and we all had our photographs taken against that.

There's a tremendous sense of comradeship and camaraderie on board; the ship's company in a submarine are incredibly close-knit, probably more close-knit than any other area of the Armed Forces. I think that being under water for weeks and months on end is more than compensated for by the sense of community and friendship that develops – we become hugely close. In fact, there are some people who are closer to their fellow shipmates than they are to their families and I have witnessed some disappointment when we're going home because people have wanted to be with their shipmates longer.

LEADING SEAMAN (TACTICAL SYSTEMS) 'CHARLIE' DRAKE

Watch-keeper in the control room, LS Drake directs his operators in compiling the tactical picture. He uses information from tactical sensors (periscope, sonar) to produce an accurate reflection of the shipping situation and tactical environment.

I joined the Navy at sixteen for standard general service but at basic training my instructor chose three from our class, and said: 'I reckon you've got the kind of mentality that goes well with submariners.' We three were quiet and got on with stuff and didn't cause much fuss within the group. 'If you're interested, I'll arrange a visit.' And I was hooked from then on in.

The first time you ever go to sea on a submarine, there's

all this anticipation and worry because you've got to learn so much at once: you've got to learn all about the sonars, the electrical, air and hydraulic systems, you've got to learn tank capacities and how a submarine ballasts, propulsion systems, and how it actually steers in the water – and you have to learn it all to a high degree and get it signed off.

I'm now a leading hand within the technical systems department. There are three of us in that section and I basically look after the lads. Our job is to create a fire-control solution and we set algorithms to achieve this. We've got different ways of getting information; daily briefs from Intel, and we have computers which give us radar information on contacts, and we also get information from electronic warfare systems, giving us bearing strength of the different radar rackets around us, commercial navigation as well as military rackets. We get a rough idea of the range of these contacts by how strong the rackets are being received by EW. It's not an exact science, but it gives a cut-off; if it goes to zero or beyond, the radar has detected a submarine mast or a submarine, so therefore we've got to make a decision about what we're going to do.

That information is passed to me from the EW, I pass it on to the officer of the watch, and the officer of the watch decides what decision to make from thereon in. If it's something like a fishing vessel with a commercial navigational radar, the likelihood is he's not going to see us, because he's not looking for us. On that premise he might talk to the captain and say: 'I wish to put a danger level of plus five,' and the captain's decision will be fed back to me and we go from there.

Your standard commercial navigation is India Band, which is the spectrum of about 9000. And then you get to Juliet Band, which is more military; usually it is pulse-compressed as well, which means instead of transmitting one pulse once, it will transmit fifty pulses all at once. The detection from that is outstanding, compared to your normal commercial India Band-type of radar.

Launching TLAMs to Afghanistan was the strangest thing in the world. We'd been alongside Devonport for about four weeks, when we suddenly got IRF-1 (Immediate Response Force 1), which means 'ready the submarine', and if anything actually happened we'd be given a job to do within a forty-eight-hour period. We were sent out to investigate a surface unit just off the coast of England. It wasn't a threat as such, so it was more of a reconnaissance, checking it out, making sure it wasn't doing anything that it shouldn't be doing.

But then the next thing we know, we're told by the captain over Main Broadcast 5 about the Twin Towers, and to make best speed for Faslane, Readiness State 1. Obviously everyone is reeling, 'Oh my God, what's happening here?' So we start making the best speed to Faslane, signal traffic every six hours up and down. As we approach Faslane, we suddenly get told: 'Carry on to Devonport.' So we crack on towards Devonport and just before we get there, we are told to go to Gibraltar. Just before Gibraltar Straits, there's another signal: 'Go alongside in Crete.' So we went alongside in Crete – oh, my God, was it ever hot there – and stocked up on TLAMs and stores for twenty-four hours. Every man carried stores onto the submarine, even the captain, and that doesn't very often happen, I'll tell you that for nothing.

It was chaos, basically. We were loading all sorts, food, dhoby gear, basically ninety days' supply so we could carry on. We didn't stop. We were pretty much out of watches. We knew we had been tasked to go somewhere and would possibly fire, but we didn't have a clue where or at what. Speculation was rife.

And then we were tasked to go straight through to the other side of Suez. We were escorted by a surface ship, with a smaller ship behind as extra protection, so we were pretty much covered in all areas. Even so, going through, you wonder, 'Is it going to kick off now?' You're really not sure.

We went all the way down through the Red Sea to station off the coast of Afghanistan as part of the Joint Task Group. One of our pumps was slightly defective, so the Americans sent out a Sea Knight helicopter, which is very similar to a Sea King, to drop off some stores. Oh, and they sent a crate of Budweiser to the captain, along with a note:

'Congratulations on becoming part of the fleet.' And he very kindly said to us, 'Stick it in the mess for the lads . . . '

We dived approximately an hour later, and within three to four hours of that we actually launched into Afghanistan. We were several hundred miles from Afghanistan, I should think. On a submarine you know certain things that are going on around the world, but you don't have internet access, so you're not fully aware of how bad things have got. But by the time we got there, we'd had a full Command brief, so we all finally knew what was happening. We are one of only a few crews who have fired in anger from a submarine. You think, This is what all the training's about, this is what we're paid to do.

We got a medal, which felt really good because, being part of the Submarine Service, you do quite a few things you don't get any recognition for, and it's nice to get some kind of formal recognition for doing your job. The medals were all sent to the ship's office, and the captain got us into his cabin one at a time and issued the medal to each of us.

I live in Bristol with my wife, Anne. We've been together for over eleven years now and we have a daughter, Lucy, who will be ten this year. She's a cheeky bugger – she definitely takes after her mum. Lucy's very tomboyish; maybe it's because she doesn't have her dad there that often, but she's doing things in a boy fashion, looking after Mum while her dad is away. But when I'm home we're inseparable; she never leaves my side, always sat around me. I go to the other room to make tea or whatever, and she'll be out there trying to help me, which is lovely. She literally clings to me the entire time I'm there, and she does the same to Anne when I'm away, which is hard for her, because sometimes she likes a bit of space.

I miss them dearly when I'm at sea, but I look at it this way: the job has its pros and cons like any job, but it means my wife can afford not to work, so she can be at home with our daughter twenty-four-seven. To me, that's a good thing.

DIY is the biggest submariner's activity at home, I'd say. I don't know why it happens, but when I am at sea something always goes wrong in the house, you can guarantee it. The day before we sailed the last time, the tiles in the bathroom lifted off the shower and the wife never got anyone in while I was away, so as soon as I got off the boat, the first thing I did was retile the bathroom. Also, the boiler packed in too, in fact the list was endless – painting, decorating, there's always something.

I have approximately two years left in the Service and I might be offered extended service for five or ten years. I'll know next year. At the moment, I'm planning to leave. Last year I resat my A-level maths, and I'm in the middle of doing A-level English. The reason I didn't get an A-level at school is because I was a lazy sod and didn't do the course work. But I absolutely love literature now; I could spend hours talking about it. Anyway, as soon as I've done that, I want to do a degree in management with a view to working in retail management. As a sixteen-year-old lad, before I joined the Navy, I worked for Virgin Games for roughly a year and thoroughly enjoyed myself. So I'd like to do that, or, I'd love to run a big store like ASDA, where there's something happening all the time.

CHIEF PETTY OFFICER TOMMY EDWARDS

As the 'wrecker', CPO Edwards and his team ensure that the ship's systems are available to support the submarine. He works long hours on the hydraulic systems but is always on hand to deal with the less pleasant duties of maintaining the heads and sewage system.

I joined up in the late 1980s. My first submarine was HMS *Repulse*, a Polaris-class missile boat, a fantastic bit of kit. It was during the Cold War and our submarines were maintained to the highest standards. I had four and a half years on that boat, and then in 1993 I joined its sister ship, *Renown*, although by then the Cold War was over and the Russians weren't putting their submarines out to sea. In my opinion, that's when things started to go downhill our end.

For instance, when I first started, you could set your clock by the way things were run. If the captain said you were going to be away for fifteen weeks, three days and two hours, then you were away for fifteen weeks, three days and two hours. When the mooring line came off and all lines were gone, that was it, we were ready for a state of war, we were fifteen minutes away from annihilating a continent. To me, they were the good times – I enjoyed every minute. Also, every day was a challenge. So for instance, if we had a mechanism with a defect that needed to be fixed, we couldn't just order one or have the submarine 'pop up' in the middle of some sea, we had to deal with it there and then and that often meant manufacturing it on our own lathes.

On board, I suppose I'm like a little Whirling Dervish or a Tasmanian devil, because I always want everything to be right first time. Right now I'm in the middle of training to be a wrecker, which is someone who maintains the hydraulic ballast systems: basically, a submarine needs air in its hydraulics in order to move and surface. And it needs to be maintained around the clock. There's four wreckers on our submarine, and we all have different watches. We spend a lot of time in the engine room and that's not easy, because you're working in ninety-degree heat; in fact, we've just had a major problem with the external hydraulics, which lasted for fifty days. But there's no point getting het up about it, you've just got to stay calm – and drink plenty of fluids.

For some unknown reason, wreckers also do all the laundry on a submarine. I don't mind, because it means we get all our laundry paid for – a bit of a perk, really.

One of the things I love about being on a submarine is the comradeship. You're a close-knit community. You live in each other's pockets. So you have to get on with everyone, because apart from your own little 'coffin', where you sleep, there's really nowhere on a submarine you can be on your own. The other thing I actually like is the fact that there are no women. As I see it, it's the last men's club, and it should stay like that.

I'd already sailed around the oceans before I met my wife, Mandy. She's a local girl from Runcorn, where I'm from. I remember the very first time I set eyes on her, I said to my friend, 'I'm in love with that girl and I'm going to marry her.' Then, when I was home on leave one time, I was going swimming and I bumped into her. And that was it. Four years later we got married. She's very good. She's a calming influence on me. She's honest, kind and gentle … a lovely woman. And she understands me; for instance, she knows that if there's anything on my mind, I'll seek out water; water has a calming effect on me. In fact, we live near the Mersey and sometimes I just drive over there and sit and look out at it, throwing in the odd stone.

Actually, I've just taken up fishing with our Graham, who's my big brother and also my best friend. He's really into fishing, and because I'd never done it before, he helped get me set up with everything, like the rods and nets. We went out night fishing when I was last back on leave, and it was as cold as a brass monkey's bollocks, but I ended up pulling in more fish than he did – not only that, but I only had one rod and he had three. And now whenever I see him, I always take the piss about that. The thing is, last year was a bad time for us – our mum and dad passed away within a couple of weeks of each other. Graham and I hadn't been very close before they died, but their deaths brought us together again and I think going fishing really helped; we got a lot off our minds.

I've got two daughters, Kerry and Kacey, and I love them to bits. Kerry's the eldest, she's coming up for thirteen in May, and my youngest is ten. Kerry's got her mother's side, very easygoing, chilled, calm, relaxed. Kacey's more like me. She's very funny; she amuses me all the time. The only thing is, Kerry was four before I went to sea, whereas Kacey's only ever known me on this job, and I think me going away affects her a lot more. On the last day before I'm due to leave, she'll go very quiet, maybe go up to her room and try and occupy herself. And then about twenty or thirty minutes before I go, I'll find her at the bottom of the stairs, crying. I'll pick her up in my arms and tell her it's not going to be for ever, and then I'll do something daft to try and make her laugh, like tell jokes or put on a silly hat.

Of course, it's a lot easier nowadays communicating with our loved ones when we're away, especially with email – although we can only do it when we surface. The captain will occasionally up the fin for crew to go out and make calls, or have a cigarette on the casing, that kind of thing. But when I started out, communication was horrendous. On bombers, all we were allowed were familygrams, forty words a week: 'Dear Tommy ... love Mandy' is four words, and you've already taken up a tenth of your letter. Not only that, but I couldn't send anything to my family, and that was for periods of four months at a time. A lot of relationships broke up as a result of that.

Actually, it's because of Mandy and the girls that I've decided I've had enough of this life. You get messed around once too often and your family get messed around too. I think one of the worst things is when they're all excited about you coming home on leave and you've literally just arrived, and you get a call saying, 'You've got to be back on the submarine tomorrow morning.' It upsets them so much. But not only that, I've also really reached a point where I feel nothing's new any more. So it's just a good time to go.

I've put in my notice and I will leave anywhere between

the next six and twelve months. I've already been offered a few jobs and I've already got my class-one wagon licence if I need to fall back on it. My annuity will pay my mortgage off, so that's one worry I won't have and, on day one of leaving, I'll also get my Navy pension. So everything will work out in the end, although I'll miss it, of course I will – there's no one on this boat who's enjoyed this life more than me.

CHEF STUART ELSTON

Chef Elston is part of the galley team responsible for preparing three meals a day for the 120 people on board.

There are around 120 people to cook for on this submarine and I'm one of three chefs. I work nights: my responsibility is to cook breakfast and prep evening meal and lunch, which includes all meat and veg, and I also make all the bread from fresh. The day chefs then make one hot and one cold meal for lunch, and two hot meals for evening dinner. We work in a small galley, which is very hot and cramped, and you've got to be careful where you put things because the slightest roll of the boat can see several hours' work land on the floor.

Normally we stock the ship the day before we sail, so everything's nice and fresh. But we're in quite a bad situation at the minute because we were alongside for the last ten days, leaving all our fresh food to just sit there. Now we're finally at sea we're having to use it up before it all goes bad – salad only lasts a week, two at the most – but luckily, veg like onions, carrots and cabbage last a good while. We try and mix fresh stuff with frozen and that way at least the frozen's not as noticeable.

For the first few weeks, the freezers are crammed with food, so nothing's easy to get at, especially if it's at the back – it's not like Tesco, where it's all on shelves, nice and neat. Last night I was in the freezer room trying to get meat out for tomorrow and it took me forty-five minutes. Then there are our dry stores, which are like holes in the wall, and it's incredibly difficult to manoeuvre around them. That's where we keep all the tinned food, so everything from tomatoes and beans to every kind of tinned fruit, plus staples like flour for all the bread and pastry-making, and long-life foods such as powdered mash if we are out of potatoes.

Our menus are very much based on naval tradition. For example, Wednesday night's always curry and Friday lunch is always fish and chips; on Saturday, it's steak, and on Sunday, there's grapefruit segments at breakfast and a roast for lunch and pizza for dinner. Tuesdays are often a themed night, so we might have Italian or Thai. Tonight we've got chicken and mushroom pie or lamb stew and dumplings – my own favourite.

To stop a sense of routine setting in with all our meals, we try and do things a bit differently, so, for example, with curries, as well as the Madras and korma, we'll also make Chinese-style and Thai-style ones, too. We always get feedback, no one's shy about telling you what they think – good or bad. The chocolate mousse last night, for example, was, unfortunately, not the best. That was foreign stuff we picked up in Crete; it's a powder you mix with milk and it's not really the best quality, but unfortunately it's on board, so it has to be used, and I think there's about two or three twenty-kilo bags of that left . . .

When we're away or I'm on leave, I like to eat out. I've been to a lot of restaurants, including well-known ones, like Jamie Oliver's. But the best food I've ever had was in a little ski chalet in the South of France. It was only bangers and mash, but there was so much attention to detail. There were four types of sausage – lamb, chicken, beef and pork – and each one had such a great flavour, the potato was proper creamy and fluffy, and the gravy was really rich. I've tried to copy it on board, but to be honest, it's difficult because we don't get the same quality of ingredients.

From a very early age, I always thought about joining up, because my dad was in the Submarine Service and I wanted to follow in his footsteps, although in actual fact, he left the year I was born, so I never actually knew him while he was in it. When he came out, him and Mum set up an off-licence and after that he became a coach driver.

When I joined up, I worked on the Vanguard boats and was on them for seven years. Then I left after I got married. I'd met my wife in South Africa, but since she moved over to the UK to be with me, I felt kind of bad leaving her in this foreign place while all her own friends and family were still back in South Africa.

But I've actually just rejoined the Service. I really missed going to sea – the lifestyle, everything. Even my wife's glad I went back. In fact, it was her idea – she could tell something wasn't right; I just wasn't my usual happy self. 'It seems like you're missing the Navy . . . ' she said.

If my wife ever asked me to leave, I'd probably consider it but, to be honest, the pay's good and, as well as paying off our wedding, which was very expensive, I'm also buying a pub at the end of the year. It's going to be a type of cock-tail bar, but also be big on food. I've already lined up the managers who will run it for me and, eventually, after I've left the Navy, I hope to look after the kitchen myself.

LIEUTENANT COMMANDER DAVID 'FILTHY' FILTNESS
Tactics and Sensors Officer

As one of two watch-leaders, Lt Cdr Filtness is responsible for leading and managing one of the two forward watches. He's responsible for the safety of the submarine over a six-hour period, and tactically manoeuvres the submarine. On the surface he is an officer of the watch, navigating the submarine from the bridge.

I was a proper Navy child. My father was in the Navy, we lived in Plymouth and then Portsmouth for a while. I was a proper naval boarding-school boy as well and then I went to university, where I was sponsored by the Navy, and then went on a fast-track scheme through Dartmouth.

When I got to my junior warfare officer's course at HMS *Dryad*, the submarine appointer turned up one day –

it turned out they were short of submariners: 'You, you and you ... you're going to be submariners,' he said. I was one of the 'yous', although I'd never seen a submarine in my life.

I felt pretty sore about that because I'd chosen to do something else on the surface, but in the end I thought, Well, it's very elite. I'll at least go and see what submarines are like. And I turned up and saw this thing and just thought, That is *very* cool ...

The biggest surprise for me about being on a submarine was how much fun it is. I joined as the correspondence/casing officer, which is the most junior of the warfare officers. You turn up without any dolphins on your number-one uniform, so you are instantly marked out as a non-submariner. Your job is to qualify first of all as a submariner, then as a ship's controller, and while you're doing all that, you're working for all your warfare qualifications, right up to becoming a navigator.

The first trip I did was across to the AUTEC (Atlantic Undersea Test and Evaluation Centre) weapons range in the Bahamas. We stayed on Cocoa Beach and Port Canaveral [both in Florida], then we went up to Norfolk, Virginia and back down to King's Bay, and then, as a grand finale, before coming home some three months later, Bermuda. And I'd been in four different five-star hotels in one month. So my first exposure to submarines was all this hot, blue water, hot weather and brilliant fun. I was a young, single lieutenant with loads of money, because I qualified halfway through the trip, and all of a sudden, the submarine pay kicked in.

I got married two years ago. I was on HMS *Vengeance*, which is one of our ballistic-missile submarines, and I proposed before a patrol and then came back with six weeks to go to the wedding.

This job has a huge effect on relationships. It's all about how well your wife or partner understands the armed forces. I'm lucky in that respect, because Becca completely understands the fact that things happen at short notice and we have to disappear. She gets quite emotional but puts a brave face on it. I don't get as emotional, but it's probably easier for the person who's going away, because you know what you're going away to and you know that actually it's going to be quite good fun.

The submarine forward divides into two, so you can manage six hours on and six hours off of continuous watch-keeping, day and night throughout the submarine's time at sea. Each of those watches is led by a watch-leader, who will always be a warfare officer. The watch system will drive the atmosphere for the rest of the submarine, so if we're doing our job well then we'll carry the whole of the submarine through. There's a joke in submarines that there are three watches: first watch, second watch – and then the other bloody watch.

My job as watch-leader is to take the submarine safely from A to B, going up and down from periscope depth, and to make sure all the submarine's daily routines are completed. I also have to learn all the warfare skills that will take me on to Perisher (the submarine command course), which I've been selected to do in June, and develop and mentor the entire watch. On a submarine, there is always someone looking after you, bringing you on in some way. The captain and executive officer are teaching me and mentoring me on tactics and sonar, and I'm mentoring other warfare officers. You could very easily be someone who just sits there and gives orders, but actually the job is about interacting with these guys, leading them and enthusing them, and making them members of a cohesive team who want to do everything together and do it well.

The watch-leader is like a conductor of an orchestra; I'm conducting the tactical systems team who are working for me forward. I'm conducting Chief Officer Barrow and his sonar team with my right hand, with my left hand I'm driving the navigation team, including whoever is on the periscope and then if I turn behind me, I'm conducting ship control as well.

Mark Alder is the MEO, the marine engineering officer responsible for delivery of propulsion, electrical systems, hydraulic systems, air systems and hotel services around the boat, which means lighting, hot water and showers. And

I've got a stopwatch running on each of those. There's a healthy rivalry between the ME department and the warfare department, but we try to get back aft and have a cup of tea with them and tell them what we're doing forward, and they come to our watch briefs and there's a good liaison between the two of us.

Navigation is a particular favourite of mine: go and have a good look at a chart and inevitably the answer is there. The feeling of the periscope cupped in your hand, turning it and seeing your target is amazing. We've got two periscopes, attack and search; the search periscope is the one which is more commonly used and has more sensors on it – HF, VHF, UHF come in through it.

But, actually, gone are the days when you're going to detect a ship through the periscope. These days you're more likely to pick up a ship using something like AIS (automatic indication system), which sees transmissions that other ships are required to make, and we also have UAP (radar) input coming through the periscope. All ships over a certain tonnage these days are fitted with a VHF transmitter that tells you their size and cargo, location, course and speed. We've had them long range in the Gulf of Aden out to 90,000 yards, which is fifty miles away, so you can detect a ship before you've even got it on sonar or seen it through the periscope. The sonars themselves will detect things out to tens of miles away. So, really, the periscope is a short-range device; you're not getting information through it directly until relatively late.

Our last watch was very busy. Joint Warrior is an exercise that happens twice a year, pulling together multinational warships, submarines and aircraft, which all come and have a play. One watch we operated with an American Ticonderoga cruiser and had a play with him; he transmitted his sonar and his helicopter came and had a look at us for a while, and then we went deep and he practised tracking us. And then the real fun started when he joined up with what we call a 'heavy', an oil tanker, a support vessel and another warship, HMS *Iron Duke*, and those three effectively had to get from A to B and we had to attack the heavy and sink the cruiser.

We conducted three very long-range attacks – one of them successful – and a lot of hard work went into that. And then during the last hour of the watch, we had to shift completely away from that into a simulated Tomahawk strike. So, three completely different serials there in one watch.

I learned never to return to periscope depth in front of a heavy and two warships. It's invariably a bad place to be because that's where they're going to be looking. I also learned that if you're going to attack something, the best place to be is either side of his escorts; he can proceed along in the direction he's going and I can just pick them off one by one as they come past. 'Spectate, don't participate,' was the key message there. It means get yourself in the right place early on, settle down and be ready early. And if that means using speed to drive yourself into position to get up to periscope depth early, then do so. Don't be in a position where you have your hand forced by an enemy because you're on the back foot – which is where I found myself the first morning. I had a Type 23 [frigate] all over me, and I had to go about evading, rather than getting the job done.

I felt very frustrated that I hadn't got it right. If I'd have given it another ten minutes, I think I would have been in just the right place, but I was impatient, partly because the captain wasn't in the control room, and I wanted to get to periscope depth and get it done without him supervising.

Anyway, the captain came into the control room and said, 'You're in the wrong place here, you're exactly where you don't want to be.' I think he actually used the phrases 'tactically inept' and 'you're going to get creamed' and, sure enough, he was right. But I've learned my lesson and I'll get it right next time. I guess that's the point.

I've done operations which are considered reasonably dangerous, but I've not been in a war. One of the things with submariners is that we very rarely get medals, because even if we've been in an area where there is conflict or combat going on, a lot of what we do is of the 'you were never there' kind of operation. People say, 'I don't want medals, dolphins are enough for me.' But actually, it would be quite nice to have a little band on the uniform that says, 'I did something useful,' so that when the Army and the RAF turn up – particularly the bloody RAF – with all their medals all over the place, you don't feel like everyone thinks you haven't done anything. Submariners are crying out to go to Afghanistan just to experience it and feel what it's like. I'd love to do an op tour, though I suspect the soldiers and Royal Marines who go out to Afghanistan regularly and do three or four tours, as they're doing now, would tell me that's a ridiculous idea.

In June I'm going on a Perisher course. Perisher is rigorous and it's pretty ruthless, too. If you fail, you're escorted to the captain's cabin, where Teacher – which is always the name for the instructor – will sit you down and say, 'I'm sorry, you haven't got it.' And he gives you a bottle of whisky. In the meantime, the submarine will be surfacing, and either a boat or a helicopter will be called in, and you'll be transferred off. While you're in with Teacher, your bag will have been packed by your fellow students and taken up top to the helicopter, and then you come out of the captain's cabin, up through the main access hatch, off the casing, and that's you, leaving an HM submarine for the last time and the Submarine Service in total. It must be a pretty horrible moment to be sat in the back of a boat on your own, seeing your last submarine disappear off into the distance . . .

There's any number of people who've failed the course who go on to be very successful ship drivers; there are a few four-ring captains at the moment who are driving large ships, frigates and destroyers, who have made very successful careers in the surface fleet, but who didn't succeed on a Perisher Course to drive a submarine. Even so, I hope I pass.

Filtness passed his Perisher course. With distinction.

LIEUTENANT MIKE GREAVES
Communications Information Systems Engineer

One of the WEO's two deputies, Lt Greaves supervises the WT office. On watch he is the fire-control officer, who operates the weapons systems (Spearfish and Tomahawk). He is also responsible for co-ordinating repairs for electrical equipment, including radar, sonar and navigational equipment.

I had always been interested in the armed forces, but I'd heard the RAF was full of posh kids, so I didn't want to do that, and Mum said she'd kill me if I joined the Army, so I was left with the Navy. Fortunately, submarines have always been an interest of mine. It's a combination of good career prospects, being under water and surviving on your own yet being part of a team. Plus, being a Yorkshireman, it was also the money.

I went to their recruitment office in Leeds and was told about an electronic engineering scheme that was open to me, and what was brilliant about this scheme was they'd pay for me to go to university. I told Mum and Dad about it and they were incredibly happy because it meant they wouldn't have to fork out so much money.

So I went to Newcastle University to do electronic engineering and what followed were the best four years of my life. It was a very busy course, but there was the whole social side of things, nights out, drinking with friends. I was captain of the rugby league team, plus living away from home and becoming independent. I'm quite an easy guy to get along with, so I had a large set of friends.

To become a submariner, the first thing you have to do is a basic engineering course. After that you join the HMS *Raleigh* Submarine School and do a very basic three-week submarine course. That's really interesting because you start learning about the systems and routines on a submarine, and you also get to visit a submarine once or twice, which is great because it allows you to see where everything is. After that, you do a six-week nuclear course, which is hard because you've got to get your head round nuclear physics – not the easiest of subjects.

When I joined my first submarine, I was flown out to Singapore and had a week there. The night before, I tried to get some sleep but to be honest, I was scared out of my mind; sure, I'd been on a submarine a few times in dry dock, but now I was actually going to be diving on one.

The next morning, the captain brought us all into the control room and told us what was going to happen. We then proceeded to dive, but the radar mast flooded, so we surfaced straight away and went back into Singapore for another day. So let's just say it wasn't the best first dive.

You never forget getting your dolphins. We had just been on an extended patrol, which meant we'd been away for eleven weeks, and this was our first time alongside. We were in Crete, where it was really hot, and the ceremony itself was held on the dock. There were six of us getting them at the same time, all lined up on the jetty, and we were told to drink this large glass of rum that had a dolphin pin at the bottom of it. We then had to catch the dolphin in our teeth and then pin it on our chests. The rum left me feeling light-headed because we hadn't drunk a drop for eleven weeks, but there were lots of celebrations that evening. In fact, I seem to remember, the drink flowed all night.

I'm now a second DWEO. I'm also the communication and information systems engineer, CISE for short. But my main role is to be in charge of the WT office, which is responsible for all the communications in and out of the submarine; in effect, we are making sure all lines of communication are available when Command needs them, and that way we are always in a position to transmit and receive signals. I'm also in charge of the crypto account, which we use for encrypting and decrypting all our information.

Some days I look in my diary and the day's been just one big defect. We have a set parameter of paragraphs, one to nine, detailing the severity of an operational deficiency. For example, alpha means you've got total loss of capability, bravo you've got significantly reduced capability, and in charlie, you've got all operational deficiencies. So say, for instance, there's a problem with the propulser, as we've recently had, that is a category B: it's quite serious because it's a noise-related defect and can affect us down the line, especially with the tasking we have at the minute. Another category B is that we've currently got a small leak on one of the valves; that means there's less steam in the pipes, which reduces the amount of power we have and affects the speed we can operate at. That could also vastly affect the ongoing programme.

At the end of the day, my job's about solving problems, and on this boat it's twenty-four hours a day. But, ultimately, I'm at my happiest when we've had a problem on board and I've taken the right course of action. I'll know when that's happened, because the captain will give us a wink and the thumbs-up.

To be honest, we work very hard when we're at sea. Trouble is, if I wake up and I'm still tired, I can be quite snappy first thing and then have a go at someone. Afterwards you're like: 'Oh no! Now I've got to work with so and so for six months,' so you're then trying to build bridges with him. But one moment you're having an argument with someone and ten minutes later you're having a wet (a cup of tea) in the mess with him. You've got to be an accommodating kind of person to be in this job, because if you're not, submarine life just wouldn't work.

One of the things I'm involved in is mentoring the guys. In fact, as a divisional officer, it's a big part of what I do. They're great guys, but they often have personal problems back home, maybe they've got a girl pregnant, or some trouble with the law, or financial problems, and I'll try and make sure I get them the best external advice, so they can go back home and sort those problems out. I hope I'm having a positive impact on their lives but, ultimately, if they can sort themselves out – or we can – it means their performance at work is better, which in the end makes my life easier, too.

I'm twenty-five now and get paid very well for my age, especially compared to all my other friends. And considering where I've come from, I've done very well for myself. My parents think what I'm doing is great and they're really happy for me and want me to go as far as I can.

I would now really like to find a nice woman, get married and start a family. At the minute I don't have a girlfriend, although I did have one for ages, but we broke up last year. Thing is, I was shoreside most of the time we were together, but going back to sea put a strain on our relationship. I was a little bit pissed off at the time when she left, but if it wasn't meant to be, it wasn't meant to be.

I actually know loads of girls but they are all up in Leeds, where I'm from, and there's never much chance these days of getting up there. Anyway, as soon as you mention the Navy thing and being away at sea, they're not really interested. As it happens, my friend Marcus has got a girlfriend called Genevieve, and she's going to try and set me up with a few people – I think she's got a particular girl in mind. My ideal girl would be Keira Knightley but, realistically speaking, I like brunettes and redheads the most. Basically, it's got to be someone who's easy-going and understanding, and takes on board that I go to sea, so she needs to have some independence.

ABLE SEAMAN (SONAR) ALEX HARRAD

AB Harrad is a junior watch-keeper in the sound room, where he monitors the sonar system to detect shipping, submarines and any other noise. On the surface he watch-keeps on the bridge as a lookout, and when going into harbour he's on the casing to handle the ropes and bollards.

I joined up to sort my life out really; I left school at sixteen and, to be honest, I didn't get amazing grades, having had all sorts of personal problems with family stuff. My mum was an alcoholic, so she couldn't look after me, and my dad, well, he was a person who shouldn't have had children. He couldn't even look after himself, really. From the age of six, I was put in foster care and started living in foster homes.

Mum was all right, she was lovely, really, but unfortunately, what I most remember was her drinking and having to carry her back home from the pub, starting when I was seven years old – I was only little. She would be in the pub every day and always when I finished school I would get the message: 'Alex, come and pick me up.' No one ever came to pick me up. So I had to walk down to the pub and sit outside with a packet of crisps and orange juice until she was ready to leave. She passed over when I was eleven, through drinking, cirrhosis of the liver, and that seems like yesterday – flown by, really. I'm twenty-four now.

I wasn't really that dedicated to school after she died. Well, you miss your mother, don't you? And it changed me as a person. I became a bit of a tearaway at school and the class clown; maybe I was seeking a certain amount of attention.

At the same time, I was moved from foster family to foster family, but that wasn't me being naughty: they would only have me for a certain length of time and then I would have to move somewhere else. I'd turn up with my suitcase in the social worker's car, and it would be, 'Oh, Alex, come on in,' and you're thinking, These people are all strangers but I am going to be living with them . . . They'd show you to your room, you'd unpack your bag, and think, I can't go downstairs yet, I don't know anybody, because I was always quite shy and by now my social worker had left. But you've got to come down in the end.

Most of them were nice. I had some cracking families and when it came time to leave, I didn't want to go, but you always got the odd couple who just did it because they got paid to have me, and some who were downright horrible. Probably the worst was when I was about eight or nine. Their eldest son was fourteen, and he must have been jealous because there was another boy in the house, and he used to pick on me big time. I'd tell the mum, but she would just say, 'Oh no, my son wouldn't do anything like that, you're lying.'

My brother Mark, he's a role model really. He was a bit like me growing up in that he went to boarding schools and stuff because of our mum, but he's a chartered accountant now, and he's got a building business too. Also, he's going to be a dad for the first time soon, and his girlfriend is really nice. I look at him and think, Well, he had the life I had, and he's sorted himself out really well, so there's no reason why I can't either.

When I was about twelve or thirteen, he didn't want me in foster care any more, so he went to social services and said he wanted to have me living with him. They told him he had to become a foster parent, so he had all the checks done to see he was a nice enough bloke to have me, and then I went to live with him for a little while.

For seven years after school I was a carer for elderly people, not a bad job, but I couldn't see doing that for the rest of my life. And then I'd suddenly had enough of not knowing what to do, so I decided to join the Navy, make new friends and sort myself out. I went to the careers office and looked at all the waiting lists, and there was an eighteen-month wait to get on surface ships, but there was a submarine I could go on with a four-month wait, so I thought, I want to get into this as quick as possible, so, all right, I'll take that.

Well, there's not much room in a sub; when you walk down the passageway you can only fit if you turn to the side, but you get used to the lack of space, and it's OK, I love it really. This boat is home for me, big time. In civvy street I had friends, but they were either people you didn't really want to be with because they were always in trouble, or people who would just use you for what you'd got. Also, my brother has his own family and obviously my mum's not here, and I couldn't live with my dad, so in a way, I feel I belong here now, and my friends on here are genuine, I get on with them so well. There's a lad called Olly Hudd, who I joined up with, and he's great; there is a tall, skinny, ginger lad back aft called Woods, and another lad called Lane, and Jameson is a good lad too, and we all seem to click and get on really well; they are family, really.

Right now I'm on basic training to be a qualified submariner. It's going all right, although it's a lot to take in, obviously, but it will be worth it in the end.

ABLE SEAMAN (SONAR) ALEX HARRAD

To get qualified I've got to learn every system on board – we've got round about thirty-two systems – and that teaches you all your electrics, how the submarine dives and surfaces, how you get air supply. Once you think you know enough about one system, you get an officer to ask you questions and, if you get stuff correct, they sign you off. I've left the hardest system to last, the hydraulics, which are very complicated, because you have your main hydraulics and your external hydraulics, and then you've got so many valves and you need to memorise where they all are and what they isolate, and there's just so much to remember.

Once you sign off all your systems, then you have the oral board, which is questions from the captain and another officer, and if you pass that, you get your dolphins and you are then qualified.

It's hard work getting your dolphins; you get some really switched-on people who remember it all in about eight days, but then it might take another person eight months. I will probably have to go at it a few times because I'm not the most intelligent person in the world, plus I'm not very mechanically minded. But I've knuckled down and I'll do it. I've done about twenty systems, which is good going really, there's one lad, the one with the skinhead, who hasn't even done one yet.

Hopefully, by the time we get back to Plymouth, I will

have got my dolphins. Apart from having my daughter Ellie, that would be the best achievement I could ever hope to have . . .

Regarding Ellie, well, to cut a long story short, I started working at a pub and met Jamie, who used to work there, and we got engaged and had Ellie, which was not planned at all, and eight months after that we split up. Since then she has married someone else. I'm all right about that, because he's a really nice bloke – he's a marine, actually, so I know my daughter's all right there, and that's all that matters really, just making sure my daughter never has a life like I had.

I have a new girlfriend called Melita: we'll get together, and then I go away to sea and worry about her. I don't think she will wait for me. She says she will and I try to believe her, but she is a good-looking girl, you see, and I've just started to think she can do better than me.

I wasn't very happy before, but joining the Navy has been a great experience and I am very happy now. There's nothing you can really do about the past, so I just look to the future. Staying in the Navy is what I most want; being at sea on a submarine is a cracking life.

LEADING ENGINEERING TECHNICIAN (WEAPONS ENGINEERING) JOHNNY 'HOPPY' HOPGOOD

Leading hand of the Bomb Shop, LET Hopgood is responsible for the maintenance of his compartment and its weapons. He also watch-keeps on the ship's systems in the control room.

I'm from Plymouth originally. When I was a kid, my bedroom window actually overlooked the dockyard and I was constantly staring out to see what was going on. My dad used to be in the Navy – he was a gunner on surface ships – and I read all his books on ships, and what really appealed to me were the stories about what it was like being on submarines during periods like the Cold War.

Eventually, I wanted to become a sailor, and the first

time I went along to the careers office, they said I'd be better off going on a submarine, because I'd get more money for it. Of course, that appealed to me, although, from talking to others who've joined up, the careers office always directs you towards areas where they've got gaps. On that occasion, there were two of us who wanted to join the submarines but there was only one vacancy, so they told us we had to sort out who'd get it between ourselves.

We said, 'Well, we both want to do this,' and we came up with this idea that the first one to move from his seat would lose the job. We sat there, waiting for the other one to give up. He gave it ten minutes, and then he said, 'Oh, sod it! I'll go then,' and went off and did aircraft engineering.

I'm now an ET WESM, which basically means I work in the Bomb Shop. My job on board is to look after the missiles, torpedoes and pyrotechnics. To load one missile takes a team of men. The way it works is you've got two Petty Officers who are the guys who give the orders to the whole team – the OA, who's the ordnance artificer, and the TI, who's the torpedo instructor. Then there's me, I'm the rear-door qualified person, and finally there's the four ETs, who are basically in charge of watching the weapon for any obstructions.

The weapon has to be lifted, moved and then loaded into a tube. They're heavy things, about a couple of tonnes each, so this is done using hydraulics, then it needs to be locked into place using air locks. There are, in fact, lots of locks and moving parts, and they all need to be checked to make sure they're out when they say they're out and in when they say they're in. The whole process from beginning to end takes about half an hour.

So, let's say you're about to fire on an enemy. It begins with the words: 'Stand by to load.' We'd then all run to our positions from forward to aft. Next I'd say, 'Ready?' and the boys on the forward band reply, 'Ready,' and make the weapon movement to panel. There's a guy at the back who operates all the power and he'll say to me: 'Rear door, you have the weapon, carry on and load to tube.' I'll then get the guy at the back to unlock the rammer and tell everyone to stand clear and load the missile.

At the moment we've got three tubes loaded with missiles and every twenty-eight days we have to take them out to inspect them. Also, every so often, we have to fire water shots from the tubes, so we can prove the system is in working order. Obviously, we don't want to do that with missiles in there, because of losing them. It's all a bit of a pain, because people actually sleep in this part of the submarine, so most of the time it looks like a hotel room. It takes about an hour just to remove everyone's beds, sheets and bags in order to give us space.

On this submarine, we're fortunate that the captain and

the XO (executive officer) like to go round speaking to the lads, find out what's going on, that kind of thing. The captain's a nice bloke, very interesting to talk to, very down to earth – unlike some captains. The one we had before was a bit of a closed book. But one thing you've got to be on a submarine, whatever rank you're at, is tolerant of other people.

When our patrols take us a long way out, contact with the outside world is very limited because you never want to give your position away. But another reason for it is that the Navy doesn't want any of us getting bad news, like someone's relation dying or something, because it's not like they can get you off the submarine in the middle of nowhere. The Navy says that in cases like that it's just better not to know at all until you're closer to home. Besides, we can't afford to have someone upset, who might subsequently lose his focus and concentration. The slightest mistake by any one of the crew could kill all of us.

The truth is you've got to be a bit nuts to want to do this kind of job because it's a strange lifestyle. You can't plan anything because you never know what you're going to be doing next, or when. I also think it's a single person's life, even though most of the lads are married. I'm single. I had a girlfriend for about nine years but we split up last July. It actually wasn't to do with the Navy, because she was used to me being at sea. In fact, she was as good as gold about that. But it goes without saying that you need someone who's willing to put up with you being away.

When it comes to finding a girl, we're like everyone else – it's usually at a bar or a club or pub. Actually, we have a term in the Navy called 'chick nicking', which is when you're out with a group of lads and you're getting on really well with a girl you've just met. The minute you go off to the toilet or the cashpoint, or wherever, the rest of the lads will try and take your girl home instead. Of course, it's just for a laugh – submariners are very good at trying to see each other off. But, having said that, one of the best things about this job is the other lads.

I've been doing this job for eleven years now, and I've done quite a lot of sea time, and as length of service equates to how much you get paid, I'm actually on quite a lot of money. I can't expect to earn a lot more at my level, but I'm dodging promotion because from what I can see, my bosses are overworked and underpaid. The POs, especially in the WE and ME, work long hours and don't get a lot of extra money for it. Not only that, but to get a promotion I'd have to do two and a half years at Portsmouth learning complicated things, including maths. I'm basically just happy doing what I'm doing, so for the time being, I'm going to stay as I am.

It always amazes me how little people know about submarines. People ask me a lot of questions about what it's like to be on a submarine: whether we've got windows, which everyone always asks, and on one group tour, someone actually asked us if our vessel was real – that was a good one!

PETTY OFFICER GORDON 'TAFF' HOWELLS

Marine Engineering Apprentice

PO Howells is one of the engineers who operates and maintains the submarine's electrical distribution machinery. He is part of the manoeuvring-room team.

I am originally from Tonyrefail in the Rhondda Valleys, a mining village, and a very famous film was made near there, *How Green Was My Valley*. But working underground wasn't for me, I didn't want to be a two-legged pit pony, as we used to call it – I was more adventurous.

As a kid, I had always been into Army Cadets; I thought the military was the way ahead. I actually joined the Army and didn't like it, so I left as a young boy of seventeen. I had a mate called Lee Jones, who was a submariner, and we went out on a session after rugby one night and he said, 'I have all

this money here, Submarine Service, why don't you join?'
And a month after leaving the Army I joined the Navy and
six weeks later I was at Raleigh Main Gate and made the
Navy my career, and haven't looked back since.

My grandfather was in the Navy in the Second World
War, and I always remember him saying he regretted he
never went on a submarine. Unfortunately, he passed away
about six months before I joined the Navy, but my Nan's
chuffed to bits, because I am the only person in my family
to join up in my generation.

My first ever submarine was *Trafalgar*. I was just about to
go on weekend leave, when literally that afternoon I had a
phone call, 'Taff, get your bag ready, you are going to sea
tonight.' I went down there, 'Hello Taff, here to join the
boat?' I said, 'Yes, where are we going?' 'Ocean wave – ten-
and-a-half-month trip around the world!' And I can't fault
it, because we went to some cracking places, like the
Philippines, America, Hong Kong, Australia. In those days
you used to stay in a hotel and they'd give you extra money,
so we would go mad, and blow off steam. We really had a
laugh.

We pulled into Port Canaveral, which is not far from
Disney World, and went over to Universal Studios, and we
drove to Daytona Beach, which was brilliant – what they
call a 'jolly' on board. The Americans loved my accent and
one good thing about the Americans is that if you are from

the British Navy – especially the Submarine Service, for some reason – they are fanatical about you, particularly after 9/11 kicked off. So, when we pulled into Norfolk, Virginia, the place was lined with loads and loads of people just coming to say thank you, and you couldn't put your hand in your pocket.

Like a lot of sailors, I am a tattoo fan. I like body art. My first ever one was the three feathers on my right arm. I wanted a tattoo to represent Wales, as I am proud of where I come from – 'God's Country', as we say. I had that done in Plymouth by a guy called Doc Price, who is a Welshman. Then in Singapore I had a Yin-Yang symbol with a pelvic sun, then a symbol of warrior and dragon to symbolise my affinity with Wales. I had a load of Celtic work done, a massive cross on my back and a Celtic design on my left arm. On my right arm I have got cherry blossoms, a massive Japanese dragon going all the way up my leg, and a big Japanese Samurai helmet and a Japanese demon mask. I also have writing on my belly: 'We sacrifice the most for the ones we love', which is true, especially in this job we do.

We went to Afghanistan in 2001. Because we were in a war situation, we didn't have much time to contact home and a lot of things happen when you don't speak to your wife, which is the sad part of this job really; many wives can't handle the husband being away. It takes a strong woman to stay with a submariner.

Ten and a half months later we returned and most of the crew were separated or divorced by then. I have seen people suicidal after one of those 'Dear John' letters, when the husbands have thought everything was hunky-dory. One of my mates had a letter come through after a mail drop saying his missus had left him, along with his kid, because she couldn't handle being left on her own. And this guy had been besotted with her. But there is nothing you can do when we are under water and locked in for weeks or months, although it's better now because we get occasional emails on board.

My wife had never been involved with a serviceman before me. First night we met, she asked me what I did and I laid my cards on the table. I said, 'This is my job, and I have got to do it for twenty-two years; I'm not leaving before my twenty-two years, so you either take me as you see me, or bye bye.' My philosophy is that my wife wants to be with me, but if she doesn't, fair enough, that's another page of my book done and dusted, and carry on. As I said, I like the Sub Service. But she has coped with it; my wife is very understanding.

I am a big family man. I have got four kids. My eldest boy, Callum, is coming up to twelve; my second eldest, Joe Benjamin, is ten; Missy Megan is five and then Hayden Michael is eighteen months old. And I've another one on the way – not bothered whether it's a boy or girl, so long as it's healthy. I'm not going to see much of their young lives, which is a challenge, but I just try and make the most of it. Before I go to sea, I spend as much time doing family things as I can, and they know Daddy is there for them.

But it is hard. Any person who says being away from his family is easy is a born liar. I have got pictures of them all on a little media drive, which flashes up their photos, and it's just nice having that homely creature comfort when you get into your rack, to lay there in your own space, and where you can say night night to them in your own little way.

I am a marine engineer technician, which is the electrical side of the engineering world. I sit in the manoeuvring room and my job is to maintain motor generators, turbo generators and the battery on board, and also the electrical distribution throughout, and look after any electrical defects that may occur.

This boat is twenty years old; it's a dinosaur in some ways. And it is like everything with wear and tear; you could have four or five weeks with nothing happening and then some weeks when your world's upside down, and you are working twenty-four-seven to get problems fixed, which is the scenario I like. I like the hands-on work, especially the big bits of equipment in the bottom. I was in the bilge yesterday for over four hours and got covered in oil. But that is why I like the engineering world: wiring up for a bilge pump, being successful, and everything is then hunky-dory.

On some submarines it is one-for-one changes, which means if a piece of machinery breaks down, they just undo the four bolts, take the unit out, put a new one in, and screw it back up – that's just the way technology is coming along in boxes now and it's easier to change the unit than actually changing the component inside. It's more economical and effective, to be honest with you. But these boats are still hands-on; you need to fix things.

It's different every time you come on watch. Some days there is a bit of lethargicness going on, and then next day it's so busy, and your watch is flying by and you think, Christ, that's gone quick. That's what the engineering life is like.

You will never see me down at sea – you have got to make the most of your time on board. I like having a laugh; I like to mess around. Practical jokes, well, you've got to, that's one of my fortes. Or, if it's quiet in the control room, I'll start doing a robotic dance. And I'll often say: 'Hey, it could be worse, fellas, we could be at home . . . '

My philosophy is work hard, play hard, especially when you go alongside and everyone gets together – you have got to blow off steam. When we are out in town, submariners are the first people at the bar having a laugh and they are always together. We were in Glasgow recently, and all the ship's company were doing stupid things on the dance floor – it is just wonderful camaraderie, there's no bitchiness, it's a great laugh. People in the nightclub were going, 'Who are these guys?' 'We're in the Navy,' we said, and they loved it.

This boat has got a very good crew on it, especially with the captain, Ed Ahlgren. I've known the boss for a while, he was my first lieutenant on HMS *Trenchant*, and he is as you see him – there's no beating around the bush with Ed, that's what I like about him. Mark Alder is my MEO and, to be honest, he is one of the very best MEOs I have ever had, which is just down to how he speaks to people and the way he is with them.

I want to get my next rate to become a chief in the Navy, and then hopefully go as warrant officer in the Watch, which is at supervisory level. But we will see. I have only got eight years left, that's all I am doing. I will do twenty-two years just to get that tick in the box to say I have joined the twenty-two-year club, and take it from there. For my job afterwards, I am looking into the nuclear power station side of things, and to have some quality time at home with my youngest, who will then be about seven or eight.

Wales is always going to be a big part of me, but the Valleys have corroded into slums and the depression and the poverty up there is high, and when I go home there is nothing to do, like when I was a kid. I now live in Plymouth, near the water, and I am into my kayaking, so we are always at the beach, and you have got big shopping centres and it is a great life for my kids – much better than my part of Wales, to be honest.

Meanwhile, I love the job I do; I love the Navy. We may not be the elite power force we used to be, but we are the best submarine service in the world and always will be.

LIEUTENANT DEAN INGRAM

As the second navigator, Lt Ingram is responsible for the safe conduct of the submarine's navigation during his two six-hour watches a day. He also acts as second officer of the watch, giving full support to Lieutenant Commander Filtness.

I went to a comprehensive school in Gloucestershire, didn't really do much academic work and left with few qualifications. But I did a lot of sport, tennis and rugby, and I competed for England in the 110-metre high hurdles. The trick to high hurdles is to stride three steps between each hurdle, otherwise you end up on the wrong foot and start clattering them; keep your hips high when you are running and pick the centre point of the hurdle.

From a very early age I was aware of the Navy. Grandfather was the chief signalman for the Fleet in the

Second World War, and when we were children we would sit round in my nan's house, which was a big farmhouse out in the country, and Granddad would tell us exciting stories about the Second World War, like the convoys to aid the Soviet Union in the war against Nazi Germany. He was part of the PQ-18 convoy, where they basically got hammered and lost over two-thirds of their ships. But Granddad got through. His journal is actually in the Museum of London now and he got the DSM [Distinguished Service Medal] for what he did.

My granddad took me down to the careers office in Bristol, just to have a look, and I joined that day, aged seventeen, even though in those days you had to do five years before you could leave. Initially I was going to be joining the destroyer HMS *Gloucester* to go on a world tour, and was really excited about that, but I got a phone call one week before, telling me it had been cancelled and I was joining HMS *Dolphin*, and going to be a submariner. So I wasn't a volunteer initially.

But it was good fun on submarines. I had good times as a junior rate and got into a whole lot of trouble – nothing serious, just drinking and high spirits. Three cans of beer per day per man was your legal allowance, McEwan's X, the red tin, I remember. But we used to store them away and save them for the weekend and if we were ashore on a Saturday night there was bound to be a fight down in the pub with the locals against whichever boat had come in, and we had some massive fights, although the next day you'd be having a beer with the guy you were fighting with the night before.

Probably one of the funniest occasions was when we were all in a pub/club type place at the top end of Helensburgh. One of our guys had had too much to drink and the bouncers handled him rather heavy-handedly, bouncing him off hard objects on the way out. So one of our lads hit a bouncer and then all the bouncers in the local area piled in and it became a mass brawl, with six of us fighting our way out of the pub. We got ourselves outside and someone asked, 'Is everybody here and safe?' and we realised we were missing one. And with that, the doors opened and this guy gets launched out, and his shirt's ripped off, he has a cigarette in his mouth, all bent up, and he's covered in blood and shards of glass and everything else. 'Right lads,' he says, 'so, where are we going next?' And that's how it used to be, that was just a normal Saturday night. Inevitably, by the end of the evening you'd get thrown into the back of the Reggy van – the Regulating Police, or the Naval Police as they're called now – and taken to the cells for the night until you'd sobered up, and eventually returned to your boat the next morning. You would then be up in front of the captain, and get two weeks' 'nines' they called it, which were extra duties and leave stoppage, and maybe you were fined, too.

And that's pretty much how it went for me the first couple of years, and not just fighting – I was late for sailing from a foreign port, which really didn't go down well. We had been in Brest for a week, partying and all the rest of it, and I went out with some of the guys the night before we sailed and was late back for sailing – they were taking off the gangway as I was turning up with my bags to get back on the submarine. I went to the captain's table again and was given the choice to either raise my papers, which means to volunteer to become an officer, or I was going to lose my PO status for being adrift under sailing orders. So I was backed into a corner.

And then, when I turned nineteen, I started to grow up, and began thinking, If I want to get on in this job, I sort of need to stop being a clown, and, fortunately, I then left that boat and that group of people.

I started doing communications and it was noted quite early on that I was good at that, and I got my rate and then I got my POs rate eighteen months later, and I finally had some sort of responsibility and enjoyed that and it was challenging. And that set me up on a path of thinking, Well, OK, I can do this. Subsequently the Navy has been really good for me, because it made me work hard, and I now have six O-levels, three A-levels and two degrees, all of which the Navy has paid for.

I didn't become an officer until five years ago. I am one

of two navigators on board the *Torbay*, so responsible for all the navigation and the planning for where the submarine goes, and making sure it's safe and it gets there on time. You can't just drive wherever you want, you have to request water from Northwood, and they will make sure there are no other submarines operating near us in that column of water. There are actually two of us here at the moment; the other submarine, which is French, is called *Perle*, and we are depth separated to stop us running into each other. She is shallow, between zero and 100 metres, and we are 150 metres down.

I met my wife Marianne at the gym through a great friend. But after about three months, I went away for over seven weeks on a bomber patrol and when I came back it was almost like starting again. I think if we hadn't had the three months before, it wouldn't have been easy, but I knew she was the person I wanted to be with, and she is now the main part of my life. The Navy is my job and I enjoy it and I'm ambitious, and there are things I want to achieve – I want to drive one of these and to be a captain, and it is, still, just possible. But if there had to be a choice between the Navy and my wife, there wouldn't be a question – I would be gone.

Marianne is very patriotic, so she is proud of what I do for a living and also of what I have achieved, but she does find it difficult when I go away, there are the old floods of tears and everything.

I would say it is actually harder for the wives than it is for us. Yes, it's hard for us to go to sea, but we are so busy when we're on board. I think about my wife every day, I've got pictures of her around my bed, but when I am here I am working. Marianne gets up every morning and I'm not there, and Marianne married me, she didn't marry the job. Wives should have the support of their husbands but for half the year or more they don't, so it's got to be difficult for them, without doubt. We had the choice; we chose to do this.

The captain is very good and approachable. This is my tenth submarine, so I have had lots of captains, including captains you can't talk to, they are just not people orientated, but this captain is such that if you have an issue you know you can have a chat with him.

The captain sensed a change in me, as I am a little bit on edge at the moment – I recently kicked off with someone in the control room over something reasonably petty and he pulled me into his cabin, I think to give me a bollocking, initially, for being a little bit fiery, 'That's not you. What's going on?' he asked. And then he sort of realised, 'Hang on . . .' and we had a little chat. I told him that just before we sailed this time, my best friend – this was the friend that introduced Marianne to me – committed suicide. It happened three weeks ago, but they only told me two days ago. I'll come home with this news fresh to me and they will have had three weeks to get used to this idea.

He asked if I wanted to talk about it, but it's one of those things I need to not think about at the moment, because it is upsetting and this isn't the place to be upset.

The longest dive I have ever done is fourteen weeks and five days. I came back and it was Christmas Eve, and I had to go Christmas shopping because I hadn't done any. So I went into town and I almost got claustrophobic; I just couldn't cope with the amount of people and everything else going on and I had to go home – I was shaking. And that was Gloucester, which is not a big town.

ABLE SEAMAN (SONAR)
ROBERT 'JENKS' JENKINSON

As a watch-keeper in the sound room, AB Jenkinson monitors the sonar system to detect shipping, submarines and any other noise made in the ocean. On the surface he watch-keeps on the bridge as a lookout and, when going into harbour, he handles the ropes and bollards on the casing.

Everybody on board knows me; if they don't, they have just joined. And everybody calls me Jenks, although at home I'm Rob.

The best thing about being at sea is obviously getting extra money, seeing foreign places, chasing other submarines. Not many other twenty-one-year-olds get to say they have done half the things I've done. The worst thing about being at sea is just being away. My girlfriend says it's breaking her heart that she hardly ever sees me; last year I was away at sea for nine months of the year and could only see her when I could get time off – a few days here, a week there – and every time I left she was in bits. So it's affecting the relationship. We have been with each other about a year, so it's not serious-serious, but it's getting there, and she wants me to leave. But given there's nothing out there at the minute, job-wise, I have said to her, 'Give it a few more years, and I will decide.'

She said she's had enough of not seeing me, and if I were a betting man, I reckon she has finished with me already. I know what's coming, I can tell by the way she speaks to me, the way she acts when I am at home. But that's life. Anyway, being tied down is not an option at the minute. I am a young guy in the Royal Navy, travelling around the world; I don't think it is the best situation, having a girlfriend, to be honest.

I have been a submariner for coming up three and half years. Oh, it's a very big deal getting your dolphins: I qualified to get my dolphins a week and a half into my first trip; I flew through my systems, because I wanted them so much. When I got my dolphins presented to me, it was a really great sensation.

They were given in the traditional way, where the captain puts his fingers in a glass and the Steward fills the rum to the top of the captain's fingers. My captain was a big guy, so that was about four inches of neat rum. The dolphins are dropped in the bottom and you must then tank it, and catch the dolphins in your teeth, and then hold the glass up to show it's empty. I had never drunk rum before – and it's rather horrible stuff.

The ceremony was around two in the afternoon, and it carried on the rest of the day and all of the night, so it got rather messy, shall we say, spending a lot of the time in the Mechanic pub, which is a naval pub just off Union Street in Plymouth, where all the clubs and pubs are. It's been there for x amount of years, and if you go round the corner, you'll see the pub is actually attached to a brewery.

I really, really like my job; this is a very happy boat. Tommy Edwards [pages 123–8] – oh my God, Tommy, he's a role model for me. He is definitely the jolliest man on the boat! You never see him with a frown on his face, even if he is knee-deep in hydraulic oil. He has had a nightmare last couple of days with external hydraulic problems, but he just laughs it off and gets on with it.

The captain keeps a very close clique with the boys and he always keeps us in the loop, which I love. Some captains like to keep themselves to themselves, but Captain Ed is constantly in the control room and chats with us, and is a very proactive captain, and likes to make his boys happy, which is a very good thing, because if it wasn't for the junior rates, the submarine couldn't run, because we operate everything on board.

To cope with living on board, you have to be very friendly, open-minded and civil; you can't fall out with anyone. It's like a brotherhood. Everybody looks after each other: 'Look after your oppo and your oppo will look after you' gets drilled into you from day one.

I did a favour for one of the lads who was getting married, but having to go to sea. He gave me a ring one day. 'Jenks,' he said, 'can you do me a massive favour?' 'Yes, of course mate, what is it?' 'I'm getting married,' he said, 'can you go to sea for me?' And I said, 'Yes, of course I can,' and I did a sea trip for him, three and a half months away.

It would be fair to say I saved the wedding, and his wife loves me to bits. They haven't got children yet, but I imagine I'm in with a pretty good shout to be godfather, if that happens. That's the type of thing we submariners do . . . if you can do a favour for people, it's much appreciated. And it's like that on board; if somebody needs something, and I've got it, even if it's something as simple as toothpaste, I'll just say, 'Right, here you go.' You help each other as much as you can.

The right attitude on a submarine is to be positive, because there are times when you will be down, when you are up off watch and you're tired. But just keep smiling and laugh things off, and you will be hunky-dory, because although one day things could be really bad, other days it will be brilliant, like a jolly, for instance. We went to Dubai, which was great, and then we went to Fujairah, and although we had been there less than forty-eight hours, we were called away early to do some special ops. Obviously, all the lads were fuming inside, because we had been at sea for months and months, and working all hours, but the main thing was that when we got back to sea, we were laughing about it. That's all you can do, because you can't exactly say, 'No, I'm not going.' Just keep smiling and go for it.

LEADING SEAMAN (COMMUNICATIONS INFORMATION SYSTEMS) CHRIS McCARTHY

LS McCarthy is watch-keeper in the WT office, where he monitors the broadcast when at periscope depth to receive incoming traffic. He is also responsible for the despatch of administrative/tactical messages released by the commanding officer.

From a very young age I have had a love of the sea. I joined the Navy when I was sixteen and left when I was eighteen, and became a tree surgeon and used to fell trees. My next job was white-lining, painting white lines down the middle of the road.

I left the Navy the first time because I thought the grass was greener on the other side, and for a long time it was, all my friends outside were doing drugs and having fun, and I was fairly wild at that stage and I enthusiastically joined in. Parties most evenings. That's part of my past now; I'm not ashamed of it, although I am not particularly proud . . . It happened.

That lasted until I woke up, and I was fat and fast approaching thirty. The white-lining companies were going downhill because it's such a cut-throat business, and I began wondering where the pension was coming from.

So, aged thirty, I joined up again and gave a big sigh of relief because to move back to the Navy, where you were pretty much looked after and had discipline imposed, was great for me, although I have always been fairly well disciplined – I have always got myself up in the morning to go to work early o'clock, and gone out and done a full day's work. It's just that when I came home, I played heavily.

I am a communicator so, basically, if we need to get orders from the outside world, they will come through me, they give me a signal and I send it off. Every vessel will have an international call sign, and ours is GBNV.

I work from an office the size of a medium-sized garden shed, which is actually a very noisy and uncomfortable place to be, full of equipment and fan noise, as it gets very, very hot there. But it's home, and I know my way around. Basically we have HF, high frequency, or what we call SSIXS, which is a satellite system, and very quick, although we are having problems with it at the moment. Generally, our primary mode of receiving stuff is through VLF [very low frequency] and HF.

We also have the signal format, CSS, which is Command support system, and we get hold of HQ through that. The Essex and Brent phones sit in the radar office, and there are two secure satellite phones.

I'm on my second marriage and, I have to say, my wife is the best. To give you an example, when we sailed on this trip, I was supposed to be fifth watch but the guy who was supposed to be going to sea in my stead became ill, and so I had twenty-four hours' notice to go to sea, so therefore my wife also had twenty-four hours' notice. And she just cracks on – with two kids of six and one. I'm very lucky, she is a very strong girl.

For the foreseeable future I'm going to be staying in the Navy because I don't think there's a great deal outside for me to do. Ten years I've got left. It's going to be a slog, partly because the money's not there to put into the boats, and we are being stretched and stretched and stretched. I'm a sailor and I realise that to make a boat work, whether it's a little boat or a big boat, you have to put money into it, and if you are not prepared to put that money in, then the boat's going to fall apart around you.

But, one way or the other, I will carry on sailing. I will never leave the sea – it's my life.

LEADING ENGINEERING TECHNICIAN (WEAPONS ENGINEERING) DANNY MANIFOLD

Using his electrical and engineering training, PO Manifold maintains vital internal communications systems on board. He also watch-keeps in the control room, operating systems such as ventilation, masts and periscopes.

I am a leading weapons engineer, and at the moment I'm responsible for the internal communications within the whole of the submarine. As well as looking after the comms, I help out the weapons lads with the sonar equipment.

I joined the Navy when I was seventeen. I don't know why, actually. I went into town with my dad to buy some trainers, and as we walked past the armed forces careers office, he said, 'Do you fancy popping in there?' I knew I wasn't really a university person, so I thought, Oh, sod it, I'll go in and have a look. And I saw a picture of a submarine, and thought, Oh, I'll do that, and I joined the Navy about a year later.

I did work beforehand. I worked on the fish counter in ASDA. I tell you what I learned in that job: how expensive monkfish is. It's ridiculous, isn't it? And tuna as well.

We did a submarine visit during our submarine qualifications. I knew it was going to be cramped from what we had been told. But when I got down there, there are pipes and valves everywhere, and I thought, How am I going to learn all this? And then, slowly but surely, you learn, and I'm still learning ten or twelve years in.

I was engaged a few years ago. But she gave me the old ultimatum, 'Right, it's either me or the Navy.' I always knew what I would do if that happened – I was going to stick with the Navy. Because you see it all the time, especially with the young lads, how they've got girlfriends when they join up, and those girls persuade them to leave the Service, and they go back outside and try to get a job, and three months down the line they have split up with the girlfriend who asked they leave the Service for them. Well, I have learned from that, and I'm glad I didn't leave the Mob for her. And ever since then, I have been reluctant to get into another relationship. I'm a happy-go-lucky type, anyway.

The best part of this job is the camaraderie between the lads. You are not allowed to be in a bad mood or pissed off in a sub because there will always be someone taking the mick out of you for that and, at the end of the day, if you make a joke of it, everything becomes light-hearted.

I still see a lot of mates from school; there's a doctor friend of mine who's doing pretty well, but apart from him, the lads are still labouring or plastering, and going down the same pubs. Actually, it's not until you leave the boat and have a weekend away from work that you appreciate how good our job is, and how good our life is. You tend not to remember all the crap, and besides, everyone has a crap day at work, even Formula 1 drivers.

So at the end of the day, I'm glad I joined the Service. And if they turned around and said, 'You have to do general service on ships,' I think I would leave the Navy. Maybe it's because we get so much more responsibility we can hold our head up higher. I'm not saying our surface counterparts are any worse than us, I just think we are an elite branch of the Navy.

ABLE SEAMAN (TACTICAL SYSTEMS) IAN 'SWAMPY' MARSH

AB Marsh collates information and uses the submarine command system to produce a tactical picture. Also, when on the surface or at periscope depth, he operates the radar.

I come from a little town in South Wales called Pontypool. My dad is an engineer and my mum works at a hair salon called Hairs and Graces.

I played semi-professional rugby as a kid, then, at sixteen, just as I was scheduled to play professionally, I hurt my back and, without telling my parents, I had an injection of steroids into my lower spine.

On my first day of professional rugby for the youth team, I walked into the dressing rooms, and they said: 'Right, you, you and you into the medical sick bay,' where a few of us were tested. A couple of days later, I tested positive for steroids, and they told me: 'You can't play for us.' I was devastated, I cried for a week – and my dad didn't speak to me for about three months. My father played professional football when he was a kid, and then he was in a car crash and smashed his legs, so he sort of had it and lost it too. So when I threw it away, he was massively upset.

Everyone in Pontypool seemed to be joining the Forces to get out, because there was no infrastructure or jobs or anything there. Me and my dad went to watch a game of football in Cardiff – when he was talking to me again – and HMS *Cardiff* was in Cardiff Bay, so we went down and had a look and I joined up then and there.

Initially I joined a mine-warfare vessel. But as the training develops they give lectures on what the Navy has to offer, and they did a presentation on submarines, and once I saw that, I was hooked. I went to my divisional officer and said I wanted to change my career to submarines. At the time there was quite a shortage, so I didn't have to do any more tests, so that was that. It just seemed to be a much better way of life: the camaraderie and the 'work hard, play hard' ethic appealed to me – as well as the pay, if I'm honest.

When I'm at sea I find myself moaning about the submarine life a lot, but then when I talk to my civilian friends, I seem to love it, so it's kind of weird. When I go home to Pontypool, a lot of my friends are in dead-end jobs, working in warehouses and factories, one of them works nights in Tesco, and some of them haven't got jobs at all. None of them are stupid, it's just that some of us snapped out of it with enough time to make amends, and some people got stuck in a rut.

Obviously my wife doesn't want me to go to sea, so she's upset when I leave home, which makes me upset, and that makes you think, I really can't be bothered. But once you get back to sea, there's another 120-odd blokes in exactly the same situation, so you pull together.

We just had three weeks off, and I said to another lad who was coming back on board with me, 'I can guarantee you will laugh more in the next three days than what you have in the last three weeks when we were at home with our wives and girlfriends.' On my submarine I am laughing from the moment I wake up, and pretty much for the next twelve hours of the day, apart from when I am in the control room on watch.

A lot of our humour is at other people's expense. There's a group of us in each watch that just sit and take the mick out of each other, and we say the stupidest things to make everyone laugh. And then you walk out of the mess and go to the control room and put your professional head on, and then go back down and just carry on laughing and joking.

You get the jokers and you get the people who are happy to sit and read a book. There's nothing wrong with that, it's just the way they cope with being at sea, but I know if I sat quietly and read a book, I would go insane. I'm one of the jokers on the boat.

It's a ridiculously tight-knit community. Something could happen on one deck, where you do something stupid, and by the time you come down to two deck in half an hour's time, the whole submarine will know you cocked up and made a fool of yourself.

Because you live in each other's pockets, you do make really strong and true friendships. There's a lad on here who's now married to my cousin Laura – I introduced them – he asked me to be best man at his wedding, and I asked him to be best man at mine. Neither of us could make it because we were both due to be at sea. But on the morning of my wedding, he rang to say: 'Is there a spare seat?' His submarine was sailing late; even his wife didn't know he was coming. I haven't seen him now for about seven months because he's been at sea on a different sub, but when I see him again, nothing will have changed.

I was out with Navy friends when I met my wife, Amy; I bumped into her in a pub in Drake, in Plymouth. We were best friends for a year, really, really close. Then when I was based in Faslane, in Scotland, I came back down to Plymouth for ten days, and we became a lot closer. After that, I did the manly thing and sent her a text message on my way back to Faslane, saying I wanted to take the relationship a step further.

Things were going fine, and then a few months later, on 29 February – leap year – she proposed to me. She rang me at about half-seven in the morning and said: 'Will you marry me?' I was like, 'Seriously?' But that was that, and we got married last July.

You get into some bad habits at sea, which the wives don't like. The big one is swearing, because obviously when you are with a load of other lads, your language can get a little bit salty and I accidentally say things in front of the wife. You don't do it intentionally; it's just that you've been sat inside a sardine can for the last few months with a bunch of blokes.

Also, the wife hates the smell of the submarine, which somehow sticks to us when we first come back. There's a little table in the porch at the front of our house, and in the top drawer there's a big bottle of Febreze, and that's just for me when I come back from sea. The moment I walk through that door, before she even gives me a kiss, she will spray me in Febreze, and then I have to go into the shower and she puts all my clothes into the laundry – even the stuff from my locker I haven't worn.

With me and my missus being best friends, we laugh constantly, and obviously I miss that. I also miss playing rugby and I miss normal food – there's nothing wrong with the chefs here, but they are just not going to cook so well for 120 people as my wife will doing it for two. And I just miss being in my new house.

Although I always talk about leaving, I never would. My wife knows I love it. And she is fantastic in that she has been really understanding about my going to sea, although I think she will be more difficult now she's pregnant. But she understands how much I regret everything that happened with my rugby career, and that I have now landed on my feet, and don't want to screw things up again.

I actually enjoy being on SMACS (submarine command system), although I like tracking warships, not sat there, bored, looking at fishing vessels. From the start it will appear on the sonar and then the sonar operators will 'cut it' – pass the information from the sonar set onto SMACS. They'll give us a time and bearing, and from that we work out speed and range to come up with a fire control solution for the captain.

You ask anyone, and they will tell you how much they hate duties. When the submarine is alongside there are about eighteen or nineteen people who have to stay on board for twenty-four hours, and that is just a waste of my life and I hate it. That alone pushes a lot of people to leave. But when you're at sea you forget all that stuff. When you think of what we do on a grand scale, we are here to do a job for queen and country and some lads are very patriotic about that. One of my really good friends is so patriotic that he toasts the queen whenever we go for a drink.

LIEUTENANT COMMANDER DARREN MASON

Second in Command or Executive Officer (XO)

Responsible for every aspect of management of the submarine, Lt Cdr Mason is a Perisher-qualified officer. At times he takes command of the submarine to allow the captain stand-down time.

When I joined the Navy, my mother made me promise I would never be a submariner. But I don't have massive regrets about joining the Service. I could have left many times, especially at a more junior stage, but you get used to the living conditions and you definitely get used to the increase in pay. What you never get used to is the separation from your family.

The Trafalgar-class submarines are the sports cars of the Royal Navy; they are fast, manoeuvrable and they get into harm's way, which is what they are designed to do. *Torbay* has got all mod cons: she is TLAM-capable, and has computerised charting and 2076, which is formidable sonar. Five years ago she was a world leader, and she's still not far off the leading edge.

Technically, she is just a lump of steel that goes into the water and does a job, but each submarine has a slightly different personality, and she is still a 'she', and she's our home.

It's been very busy at the moment, and there are not enough racks, so we have twenty-two people hot-bunking, but the ship's company is strong and united, and that's reflected in how many people are remaining in the Service. I think if we were a weaker bunch of people, we'd all be leaving.

I spent seven years of my life being a sonar officer, so you could say that was my specialty, but I also did five years being a navigator, and I've passed Perisher: my whole career has been about providing me with sufficient strength and depth of knowledge of all those positions. My role at war is attack coordinator, and my dedicated function then is to provide the captain with the fire-control solution; it is my job to ensure that every time he wants to fire a torpedo, I have given him the ability to do it. Only the executive officer and the captain have weapons release, although the officer of the watch has permission to counter-fire, which means if someone was firing on him, he has permission to fire back.

Perisher is a command course, not a practical course, so if you fail Perisher, it's because you couldn't make command decisions and lead. And if you fail, you are not allowed to come back, so basically your career in submarines has come to the end of the road. One guy took himself off the course about ten days in, another was removed on the day before the end of it – I think he was beginning to doubt himself – and it was sad to see him go, he is a friend, but unfortunately it had become clear he wasn't destined for sub command.

Perisher's sea phase is pretty intense. You're stealing about two to three hours broken sleep a day until you find your core strengths and then you must find an ability to deal with complete and utter fatigue. Also, you must have the ability to drive people to do what you want them to do. When things go wrong, the boys look to you and expect you to man up and make a decision. It might not necessarily be the right decision, but just come out with a decision that is structurally sound, then have the grace to adapt your plan on secondary information.

Because of Perisher, I have become a lot more focused and much more aware of who I am and what I can do.

In normal running, my role as the executive officer is to support the tasking. So I make sure there is sufficient training, sufficient manpower and sufficient food, and that the other heads of department work together to do the captain's bidding. At the same time, I have a secondary role as second in command, and when we are very busy, the captain will share the submarine with me. So I am doing my core job, then I am allowing him sufficient down-time so he can get a bit of sleep, and he knows that during those six hours we are not going to do anything stupid.

Also, as head of the executive department and head of the warfare department, I am a mentor to the officers, and I write their reports and manage their lives. I was recently able to get one officer home to see the birth of his child. I didn't have the opportunity to be there when my children were born and that experience made me realise how important it is to be there. So I made a large effort, although it was relatively easy with this captain – he didn't take a great deal of convincing.

What we do in the submarine is inherently dangerous. We live inside a steel tube seventy to eighty metres below the sea, so we don't have a great opportunity for escape, and all our lives are dependent on the weakest link: if the most inexperienced person makes the most innocent of mistakes, he could kill us all, and that's a risk we have to live with. So, without sounding condescending, we, the experienced people, are always watching to make sure the most junior people don't make mistakes, and there is constant mentoring to make sure they learn the correct way to do things. And that's why we demand such exacting standards.

Hopefully, the submarine is relatively clean and tidy, and that discipline builds on to how we as a company present ourselves. I will not tolerate poor drills. If we let our standards drop, people start cutting corners, which, ultimately, means people could die.

I've never fired at a ship or sunk a ship and I hope I don't have to, but if it comes to it, then I will do my job. Do I expect to go to war? Yes. We will definitely be involved somehow, somewhere. I would die for my queen, although I would obviously prefer not to, but I'm prepared to. You have to be willing to lay your life on the line in this job, and you may as well die for something you believe in. I believe the UK is the best country in the world. I also believe that my government won't go and do something completely stupid and send us off on some daft witch-hunt, so there's a level of trust there.

Because we're an island, the Navy has a vital role, even in peacetime. Perhaps people are naive as to how important the sea lanes are to us, and how important it is we police them. We only have eleven submarines, of which seven are running, and people know nothing about them, nor understand how they work. For example, undoubtedly the most common question we get asked is, 'Do you have windows?'

Big ships are very big statements of power, but the Submarine Service has always been the silent service: we have the motto, 'We come unseen, we do our bidding, we come back.' I don't get upset that the general public doesn't know what we do because I know we make a difference. But, deep down, all of us would like to have the bunting coming out when we come home, the heroes' welcome and all that. But I wouldn't want to take away from the Army for what they do in Afghanistan because that's proper nasty living. We have our own hardships here: no space, no air, no families, no leave, crap food and all sorts of stuff, but at least I am not being shot at, so there's no doubt the Army deserves all the kudos it gets.

I am very fortunate that my wife is from a military family; her grandfather was in the Navy, and her father was in the RAF. But we don't spend a great deal of time together, which is a huge wrench and has a dramatic effect on my family life. We have got two young kids and I don't see them as much as I would like, that's for certain. It's upsetting, especially when you hear they are worrying about when you are coming home. Children expect you to be around the corner and you're not.

You would struggle to find anyone on the submarine who doesn't miss their family – everybody's got lovely families. The problem is that when you don't see them your lives diverge and, unfortunately, a lot of marriages fail. It's a sad fact that we all know more about our fellow officers than their wives do. I see my wife forty to fifty days of the year, but I spend three hundred days of the year with my colleagues, so by definition you are going to know them better. But if Ruth said to me, 'I need you to leave the Service, because I can't cope any more,' there wouldn't be a second's hesitation. You know the old cliché – live to work or work to live? There's no doubt in my mind which way it is.

When I'm away, Ruth has to be the man and the woman of the house. We live in Devon, and Ruth's and my families live in Sussex, so there's not a great deal of support. She is a single mum in a four-bedroom house, which is paid for by her husband, who is at sea, and that's pretty much the be-all and end-all. When I come home there's always a difficult balance of power, because she's not used to me trying to be the commanding officer of the house.

It's the best thing in the world to see my children again, it's happiness personified. You come home and your one-year-old son is now almost one and a half, and he has changed dramatically. But you've got children who aren't used to a male voice in the house telling them off; my mischievous three-year-old son is most definitely pushing his luck at the moment. So, generally speaking, after a very short honeymoon period, the kids distance themselves from you because they are punishing you for being away, which is very sad.

CHIEF PETTY OFFICER
(TACTICAL SYSTEMS)
ALLAN MAWBY

As the senior rate in charge of the tactical systems section, CPO Mawby is responsible for monitoring the production of the tactical picture (see Charlie Drake, pages 115–121). At Action Stations, he sits in the OPS seat and co-ordinates the picture himself, producing the best tactical assessment so that weapons can be used successfully.

I'm called 'Chops' by the lads, which is short for Chief Ops; there are two of us Chops on the boat: I'm Chief Ops TS (Tactical Systems), and Richie Barrow is Chief Ops S (Sonar). Basically, my job is to compile a picture of what's going on around the boat. I've got to bring together all the information possible, whether it's from the sound room, electronic warfare, or the visual information available from periscopes, and then give it to Command, so he's then in a position to avoid what we need to avoid, or put a weapon in the water and sink what we need to sink.

Some contacts we can pick up miles away on sonar, and some we can't, in which case the contact comes through on visual first via the periscope. So it's basically about putting all these clues together to get a full picture.

When I first started out in the submarine world, I was on the diesel–electrics, which were a different ball game from these Trafalgar–class boats. For a start, the entire trip, there was no showering or anywhere to wash your clothes; also there was a lack of fresh food, so it wasn't uncommon to find yourself eating mouldy bread, and when it came to sleeping, the beds were so small, you'd struggle to get into them. And finally, if you were on the surface and the weather was bad, you'd be rolling about all over the place. So it was a tough life, but they were good times, and the crew was even tighter than this one.

We seemed to spend less time submerged in those days, one minute you'd be at sea, and the next minute you would be pulling into a port and parking there for the night. I went to places like Tenerife, the Falklands, America, Norway and Russia. The time we were in Russia, we pulled into Severomorsk, just north of Murmansk. The people were very friendly and helpful, and although they had very little, they gave us what they could. They watched out for us, too. I'll never forget, I was opening a bottle of vodka when this lady came up to me and knocked it clean out of my hand, and in quite good English she said: 'Don't drink that, it will make you blind.'

I'm actually not one for sitting in bars all day. I prefer to see a bit of the culture, walk around the streets, pop in and out of shops. I remember going into a butcher shop in Murmansk and the stench was awful; another thing I noticed was that the cleanliness of the toilets wasn't too brilliant.

I probably liked Norway the best. I've now been to the city of Tromsø twice, and the people there are nice, and the scenery is lovely. You get a great panoramic view of the city if you take a cable car to the top of Mount Storsteinen, one of the mountains overlooking the city. I also went to the Arctic Cathedral, which is a white, bow-shaped, modern building, and there's a museum dedicated to seal hunters, which took my fancy. For some time now I've been threatening to take the wife on a cruise of the Norwegian fjords; I actually think she'd love it.

Me and my wife, Paula, met at school, we were even in the same class. We're from Liskeard in Cornwall. The nicest things about Paula are that she's dependable, reliable, always there, and very sensible – never spends my money – a typical farmer's daughter. We've been married now for nearly seven years and we've got two kids, one's four and the other is two. To be honest with you, I find it hard leaving them for any length of time. When my youngest son was about nine months old, I was away for about three and a half months, and when I came back, I noticed such a difference – his face, his attitude, the way he had become so grown up in his speaking. Now, I can see it happening again with my youngest when I have access to Skype.

Going away from your family is hard, I end up thinking about them all the time. Some people can put it to the back of their minds, but I can't. On the boat, there's a few of us who talk about our families. The wife of one of my lads is pregnant and he asks me questions, and I like to give him hints and tips on how life's going to completely change, although actually, he's a quite sensible lad. I also talk about things that have happened to me, like the time I was due to go to sea and my missus had a miscarriage, so I didn't go. One of the officers on board has just had a kiddie and I think he's missing his wife. If I were a young chap with a young family I'd probably seriously think about giving it up.

When I'm at home, I'm involved in so many activities. I'm currently the vice-president of the Liskeard Lions, which is similar to the Rotary Club. We raise money and give it to local and international charities, whether it's disabled or underprivileged kids, or international disasters, like the Haiti and tsunami appeals. It involves dinners with all the other districts in Cornwall, like Saltash, Tor Point and Launceston, but they're real bow-tie affairs and, to be honest, that's not really me. In July I'm taking over as the club's president, and I'm pooing myself because later in the summer we have the Liskeard Parade, which is a floral procession, and I've got to be at the front of it. Everyone in the town will be watching me, and there are dance steps you've got to learn, and I can't dance, so I'm not looking forward to that. And my wife's cursing me out because she's got to do it all with me.

One of my favourite pastimes is fly-fishing. My dad enjoys it too, so he'll often come with me. I have to get to somewhere quiet, away from people, so we'll often go down to Black Lake, which is quite near us. Dad's usually a couple of hundred feet away from me, and there's always a bit of competition between us as to who can catch the first fish or the biggest fish. But sometimes I don't even care if I don't catch anything, because it's so nice just to sit there, watching the wildlife go by all day – kingfishers, herons – it's where I'm happiest.

I have to confess that sometimes when I'm at home, I stop and think, What am I doing in the Navy? Luckily for me, my career is coming to an end now, I've only got another two years to go, so the boat I'm on now will probably be my last one. I know I'll miss her and being in the Navy, and when I walk off *Torbay* for the very last time there might well be a little tear in my eye . . .

CHIEF PETTY OFFICER JOE METHVEN

Heading the forward staff, CPO Methven undertakes the same duties as the wrecker. He is also responsible for the maintenance and availability of all fire-fighting equipment. He sits at the ship's control console (commonly known as the panel) where he controls the movement of major hull valves, the trim, bilge and ballast systems, the masts and periscopes and the hydraulic and high-pressure air systems.

I basically had no choice. As I was in the top 2 per cent out of my entry I was selected for Submarine Service: top of the class meant submarines in those days. At the time I was pretty pissed off, because I lived on the Isle of Wight and had asked for anything floating out of Portsmouth – and I got sent to Faslane, best part of six hundred miles away in Scotland, on a bomber, as the SSBN (Vanguard class) boats are sometimes called. So, a bit of a culture shock. But once you do submarines, you are not doing anything else. It's a wonderful life, with camaraderie and respect: if I say something to the captain or an officer, they'll take my word for it, whereas in the general service it's not the same.

Obviously my parents and wife are proud as punch for what I do, but they don't really have a great understanding of what sort of life we submariners have. They find it rather strange that people like to bimble around in a bean tin. The thing is, there's not very many of us around – we are a different breed, really.

I'm basically in charge and look after every system on this submarine that doesn't involve us propelling through the water or picking up weapons: all the water, trim, bilge, ballast, hydraulics, all the galley equipment, the domestic equipment, the heads, the bathrooms, the steering, the hydroplanes, the escape, and the fire-fighting. And every single one of these systems gives me gyp. *Torbay* is old and tired, and it's a constant battle at the moment just to keep her going. She needs a rest.

This trip the hydraulics have played up immensely; we set up pump baling, but now metal has got round the system. Also, I've got my eye on all the air-ventilation systems, and I have particular worries about the induction system, which is not draining down correctly, and we have a problem with our foreplanes. But we keep on running and running her. We wouldn't be at sea now if she was mine.

My life outside is totally different when I get away. I live in a little cottage just outside Falmouth, and eleven weeks ago I had a little lad, called Zachary. Got what I wanted, a little boy, and that's it.

So that's pretty much taking up most of my time. I would like to get out and play golf, but unfortunately my wife has got horses, so I have to get involved with that, help her ride the horses and take them to all these shows, which isn't my best enjoyment. I don't like horses.

I used to love this job – it was so much fun, with so many laughs. Obviously, with cuts in pay, and all the rest of it, it's not what it used to be. I used to really enjoy runs ashore. There's not many runs ashore to non-naval ports now; our last fun one was about five or six years ago in America, a dim and distant memory, unfortunately. It's just work, work, work.

This is my twenty-first year in the Submarine Service, but I have just signed on for another ten years, on account of having the little lad, because there is nothing outside for anybody, let alone with my particular skills. So, another ten years of this. I'll be fifty then, so that will be it, no more.

ABLE SEAMAN (SONAR) GRAHAM 'GOOCH' PARRY

A junior watch-keeper in the sound room, AB Parry monitors the sonar system to detect shipping, submarines and any other noise made in the ocean. He's trained to determine the number of shafts and blades a ship might have by listening to its signature. On the surface he watch-keeps on the bridge as a lookout and, when going into harbour, he is on the casing to handle the ropes and bollards.

To be completely honest, when I went to the careers office, the job I really wanted was aircraft handler; I'd seen a TV programme on Channel 5 called *Warship*, and just thought that looked really cool, and would be like *Top Gun*. But they went: 'There's a twenty-four month waiting list for that,' and I thought, Heck, no, I'm not waiting that long.

So they said, 'How about seaman specialist?' But that had a waiting list of eighteen months. And then, finally, they said: 'Have you ever thought about working on submarines? They're the Navy elite, you get paid a lot more than anyone else, and you go on jollies.' But actually, the submarine episode was the one episode on the TV series where I thought, No, no, no, I'm not doing that. That looks rubbish.

The thing is, I was working at Currys as a salesman and going absolutely nowhere. There was one person who would hammer me every day as if he had nothing better to do: if there was a toilet to be cleaned, he'd make me do it, even if I'd done it for the last four days in a row. So, anyway, that made me think, Right. Submariner. Gonna go for that . . .

The day I passed out was the proudest day of my life, throwing my cap in the air, and seeing my mum crying with pride, I loved all that. But there were times along the way when I thought, Oh God, what have I done? I did eighteen weeks' sonar training and kept worrying, 'I can't remember these frequencies, this is very hard,' and I was getting to the point where I was like, 'I've made a big mistake. This is crap.' I got through it eventually, but SMQ was the hardest thing I've ever done, because it was very academic, and I'm not an academic person. Also, my on-off girlfriend phoned just before the exam and said she was really ill, and after that I didn't sleep all night and failed the exam, and then I had to go on leave for ten days, because I couldn't cope. But she was all right in the end, and I passed the exams later on and joined the boat.

I'm now a sonar submariner. My job is to maintain an overall picture of where we are and monitor what contacts we have by sound, be they fishing vessels, merchant vessels, warships or other submarines. Fishing vessels make a trawling noise, they sound like clanking metal, so if I hear that, I know to stay as far out of its way as possible. There's a lot of 'bio': you can hear whales most days, plus shrimp and dolphins, which sound like little crackles. Some of the time that's interesting, but most of the time it is quite dull.

This last time on the submarine has been a bit swings and roundabouts, some days I am all right, then others I'm not. I spent my twenty-first birthday on board and I remember looking at the clock turning to midnight, and I just thought, I'm here on my twenty-first birthday, on board a submarine on a Saturday night, when I should be out celebrating, and I was just livid.

I haven't once woken up thinking, I'm happy to be here, but I've had a lot of those 'What have I done? What am I doing here?' moments. I know I'm only twenty-one, but if I stay in for four more years, I'll be twenty-five and that isn't so young. I regret joining this particular branch, simply because it doesn't interest me. Actually, I've always wanted to be a policeman, that'd suit me much better. I've also thought about the RAF, because I've seen jobs I am interested in, but it's not as much money because submariners do get paid quite a lot compared to everyone else, although at the moment I'd rather be happy than have all that money because money isn't everything.

So I've been borderline depressed about how much I don't like it on board and how hard a time I'm having, and I got to the point where I didn't want to be on a submarine. So I wrote this letter and signed it and gave it to the Chops, who then gave it to the TASO, who then passed it on to the captain – I certainly didn't expect it to go that far.

The captain called me up to his cabin. I was really nervous. I thought he was either going to say 'Man up and stop being a baby' or 'Sorry. There's nothing I can do.' But he was very sympathetic to how I felt, and he called up inboard and it turned out there was potential for me to change to seaman specialist. But I thought, No, leave it, I'm going to stay sonar. I sent the captain an email thanking him for his time, because I really appreciated it, and said, 'I'm going to stick with this job.' Apparently he was very happy with that.

But I won't lie, most days since then, I've thought, Damn. Should have gone skimmer. But the money is important and you have to think about things like that. Also, as other people have said to me, it's probably a case of the grass always being greener somewhere else, and that may be true. If I was working on the surface, I would probably be painting ships most days and maybe throwing the odd heaving line.

So I reckon I'll stick with this for the minimum of four years and then see where life takes me.

LEADING LOGISTICIAN
(SUPPLY CHAIN) B.J. POTTS

LL Potts is responsible for monitoring the vast volume of stores going to and from the submarine, ranging from items for long-planned maintenance as well as materials for immediate repairs that will allow the submarine to sail. His secondary duties include acting as planesman at sea.

I am the leading stores assistant. Basically, I am like a Tesco delivery driver; I get everything that is needed by the engineers and mechanics from our three depots in Portsmouth, Plymouth and Faslane, really boring stuff like gaskets, screws and electrical cards. It's just a simple, computerised system . . . I could go into it more, but it would really send you to sleep.

I was brought up in a little town called Buckingham,

near Milton Keynes, which is one of the furthest cities away from the sea in the whole of the UK. I left school when I was eighteen, after my A-Levels, and for a year I worked as the first point of contact in the complaints department of Equitable Life. I joined literally a month before the whole situation with everybody's pension pots going down, and people in their eighties and nineties, who had lost tens of thousands of pounds, were calling me in despair, which was very depressing.

But my stepdad had been in the Merchant Navy, and listening to his stories about travelling round the world when he was younger drew me into thoughts of a Naval career. There wasn't actually a Naval career centre in Milton Keynes; it was all Army. So I went to the nearest Naval careers office and we had a little chat. 'Do you want to join the Submarine Service?' they asked, and I said, 'Not really, no.' 'OK, sign this form here,' they said. I signed it, and I guess that form went into a bin somewhere, because at the end of the course they said, 'We need some volunteers for the Submarine Service because we are really short, and if you don't volunteer, we will volunteer you.' So me and a few others put our hands up and volunteered. I just thought, Yes, I'll go for it, as I'm not normally in the habit of making devastatingly bad decisions. And everything good in my life started from that moment, really.

After I did my submarine qualifications, I joined *Torbay*

and the week after that I met my now wife. About fifty of us went out on a mess night to this fantastic, massive wine bar called Club Jesters in Union Street in Plymouth. There's a Trafalgar submarine bar in the back where we always seem to end up. And to be honest, I don't really know what happened that night. Fate, I suppose, but we were both very tipsy and sort of bumped into each other on the dance floor, and that was it.

About four weeks later I went to sea for three months, came back, and we somehow ended up living together, and then two years later we got married and I've now got two little girls.

Although a lot of it can get quite repetitive, I enjoy most parts of my job, but most of all I love the banter, and the way we all get on together on this submarine. There are always lots of fun things going on. The best jolly was when we stopped off in Crete last year. Me and my AB (Able Seaman) had to fly out a week before the boat got in to do a logistical support, so we had an extra week by the swimming pool, which was really good fun. Unfortunately for the rest of the guys, they got bounced and had to sail early, so they only had a couple of days.

I've got my rate, my Killicks, which I'm proud to wear, and I hope to get promoted again, but the long-term plan after that is I'm looking at emigrating to New Zealand and joining the Royal New Zealand Navy. I want a better quality of life. I want an orange tree in my garden. And I think my wife has been persuaded by the idea of being close to a beach, the hot, sunny Christmases and giving the children a better upbringing than they are able to have in this country.

So I am very open to different challenges and I'm looking forward to the future.

LEADING STEWARD IAN PREVOST

The leading steward managing the wardroom, LS Prevost also runs the submarine's central fund (non-public money). He's also a planesman, driving the submarine, and he's in the first-aid team – he's the first on the scene of a fire in breathing apparatus.

I'm the senior leading seaman on board – you can't get any higher than me. I'm the captain's personal steward and I look after him in every way he wants, feeding him, getting his uniform ready, making sure he's in the right place at the right time. I've served with Captain Ed before, when he was the XO, so I already know his likes and dislikes. He's the easiest commanding officer I've ever had to look after: he hates fish, loves chicken, cheese rolls and pasta.

One of my other jobs on board is treasurer of the messes'

bank accounts, and I help run the canteen, buying and controlling the stock, and paying all the bills; I also form part of the medical party on board, and I'm a planesman.

After nineteen years in the Navy, the standard of life on board has changed so much. When I first joined submarines, I wasn't allowed in the mess until I became a submariner, and I got, if I was lucky, three hours' sleep a day. With the old system they'd learn respect for their elders and would also understand things a lot more. Now we're not allowed to beat them up – they're mollycoddled; but that's the Armed Forces throughout now, and life.

I'd done a lot of jobs in civvy street before joining the Navy. I started off my career as a butcher and qualified as a master butcher at the age of twenty. I was lucky, I learned from a well-established family that had a dozen shops in south London, and I learned my trade off a ninety-year-old master butcher.

I had to learn everything to do with preparing meat, from taking it from the field to the abattoir and putting it on your plate: I learned how to slaughter, how to hang the meat and prepare it for retail sale to butchers, and then learned how to cut the various cuts of meat. My personal favourite cut is tail-end skirt, the fillet; once it's cooked properly, it's really nice and tender. You can't buy that any more. Most butchers sell it as skirt and therefore it gets put in beef burgers, and supermarket butchers don't even know about it. Most of the younger-generation butchers coming through now don't understand meat, they just get taught: cut here, here and here.

I went from being a butcher to working in a hotel attached to Happy Eater 001, the first-ever Happy Eater in the country, so quite a lot of history there. When the hotel trade took a bit of a dive I had enough of that and I went to the careers office and said, 'Where do I sign?' I knew I wanted to go into the Navy: stability, guaranteed money and a chance to see the world. But it's funny, because I used to suffer from seasickness: my parents took me on a ferry one day and I did nothing but throw up.

My first submarine was *Tireless*. I just loved the way of life. After I got my dolphins I loved it even more, because, to put it bluntly, I wasn't treated like shit any more, I was given respect because I was now a member of the club. If you're ever lucky enough to see a dolphin presentation, you'll hear the captain say, 'You are about to join the most unique club in the world, it's blood, sweat and tears that makes you a member of this club, not anyone can join it, it doesn't matter how much money you've got.'

My first love will always be *Tireless* because it's the boat I learned how to be a submariner on. The saying is, 'You always remember your first boat,' because you know everything about it. My next boat was *Talent*; I had seven years on that and I brought it out of refit, took it through work-up, and it's where I met the captain, and we've got some tales between us of what happened there. I'm one of the fortunate people who has been on all seven Trafalgar-class submarines: I've also had one bomber, two U-boats and three P-class and O-class boats, so I've had a varied cross-section of submarines.

I met my wife on shore leave up in Scotland. There was a club called the Drumbeat Club and some football thing was on the TV. Well, I hate football with a passion: it's twenty-two blokes running around a pitch and if they score a goal they go around hugging and kissing each other, and if they just get tapped they cry. Sorry – be a proper man, play rugby: blood, snot, tears, broken bones and teeth, but they still carry on playing and then they shake hands.

Anyway, I got a little bit illubriated during that match, and it was, 'Oh, all right, let's have a dance,' with this girl I spotted, but it was basically love at first sight for the pair of us. I proposed to her not long after on the concrete steps of Sainsbury's car park in Plymouth, after being in the RNA all afternoon – the Royal Naval Arms. I was very pissed, and she said, 'I'm not going to say "No", but if you remember in the morning, ask me again.' I woke up in the morning, and said, 'I asked you a question last night. I'm asking you again – will you marry me?' And she said, 'Yes.'

I'm very lucky with Suzanne, because her father used to be in the Navy so she's used to the naval life of loved ones being away, so there's no problem there, although she hates it when I'm away, especially now we've got two kids. But that's life. I earn the money to give them a roof over their heads and I ask for nothing and I'll give them everything; it's just the way I am. But it's hard saying goodbye to the kids. My son turned five Tuesday last week, while we were at sea, and I've only been home for one of his birthdays. I saw my daughter when she was six days old and stayed for just four days before I was back at sea again.

I generally don't talk to my wife for the first fortnight of being away, as I'm trying to get my head around being at sea. My wife and the kids are now the most important thing in my life and this submarine is a job; I still love it, but it used to be an adventure, and now I can't wait to get home to see my wife and kids again and have what slightly resembles a life for a couple of weeks before we go back to sea. I'll normally get home very late at night when the wife and kids are fast asleep, so I'll get in and curl up on the settee and wait for the kids to come and wake me up in the morning.

Well, I leave the Navy in two years' time, when I'll be forty-two, so, just in time to start a second career. I'm looking forward to a new challenge, I've already got two jobs lined up. One of them is working for St John Ambulance, as I'm a trained St John Ambulance technician and emergency driver. I'm also a qualified civil book-keeper, so I can go into book-keeping. With my experience of running central fund, I've already been told by one accountancy firm in Plymouth that they will gladly have me, on account of my training within the Navy, because in civilian street you're allowed up to 10 per cent errors, up or down, and in the Navy you're allowed zero errors.

Torbay has been a brilliant boat; I've been places I never thought I'd go. I've been east of Suez a couple of times now, and would have liked to have gone further east with it, possibly circumnavigate the world, as we were supposed to do, but didn't. The boat itself has got its problems; she is old but she will carry on going, no matter what, because the crew will make sure she keeps on going. You've heard the phrase, 'a sleek, black messenger of death'? Well, that's exactly what we are, a sleek, black messenger of death. That's what we do best. We will go in, get the intel and blow ships out of the water. They don't know where we are, but we know where they are, though, they make so much noise it's unbelievable. We find them, and blow them out the water, and then Oscar, Oscar, Whiskey.

I must admit, I will have a tear when I leave here, because it will more than likely be my last time on a submarine, or at sea, full stop. But it's the same for everyone: you have to know when your time's up.

ENGINEERING TECHNICIAN (WEAPONS ENGINEERING) DEAN REILLY

A member of the Bomb Shop team, AB Reilly is involved in the maintenance of the heavyweight torpedoes and cruise missiles on board. He also watch-keeps in the control room, operating the ship's systems such as ventilation, masts and periscopes.

My family used to be travellers, but when my mum split with my dad, she moved into a house and got a job as a cleaner. I saw my dad about five times before I was fifteen. He's a nice person, sound as hell, but just don't expect a Christmas or birthday present from him. I've got a big family. My nan's got nine kids, I think, so there's too many cousins to count. But I don't really connect with them – they try to put me down because I'm not a traveller. *Gorger,* they call me, which means I live in a house. I hate travellers. They're so arrogant. I say to them: 'What have you done with your life? Learnt how to block-pave a drive?' I think I was brought up a better way.

I did well in school. Could have been a A-plus sort of student, but I had my mind set on plumbing or plastering and ended up doing a plumbing apprenticeship.

I got good at plastering and started working at it on the weekends with my brother-in-law. He offered me a job at £100 a day. 'Work as many days as you want,' he said. So I picked Monday, Tuesday and Wednesday, and that was ideal, £300 for three days, which was way more money than anyone else my age was getting, and not far off a grown man's wages. But then on the Thursday, Friday and the weekend, I was bored, so I started doing a lot of drinking and gambling, and by the end of it, I needed to sort my life out because it was going nowhere.

My mum always wanted the Navy for me and she sat me down one day and said: 'Why don't you give it a go?' She'd already looked into it and knew I could get out within six months if I didn't like it. Also, she thought it would get me away from the people I was hanging round with. I've never had a criminal record, but I wasn't far off it. And the drinking was getting bad: sometimes I'd be so pissed, I'd wake up and all my money was gone, which wasn't the best state to be in. So I thought, Yeah, OK, I'll give the Navy a go . . .

ENGINEERING TECHNICIAN (WEAPONS ENGINEERING) DEAN REILLY

I was set to become an AET, an air engineer technician, because my granddad was one in the Second World War, but I failed a colour-blindness test, so they said: 'Do you want to go down and visit a submarine?' It was a Thursday and I had a day off, so I went down and it looked all right. So I thought, OK, I'll give it a go, and I didn't really stop to think: Would I enjoy it? I was just set on completing the tests, proving that I could do it. I saw it as a challenge and that's how it's been ever since. Everyone was dead proud when I eventually qualified – Mum cried when she heard the news – and I joined the boat about a year and a half ago.

But now I'm set on leaving the Navy and going outside; I want to move on with my life. One of the major reasons is because we get told to clean way too much. You expect that, but to put in a six-hour shift and then have another couple of hours to clean, and then get told, 'It's not good enough,' is too much. Also, they've taken the PlayStation 3 out of our mess. I'm twenty-three! I don't want stuff took off me – I consider myself an adult now, a man. I don't wanna be back in school where they say you're not working hard enough, and so you're not allowed this or that. It's very dispiriting, and it lowers morale. On the other hand, after they said we had to put more effort into our cleaning, you really see the junior rates' mess coming together as a team, and that's a good feeling.

When I was working three days a week, I couldn't even be bothered to get up some days, so I haven't regretted my time in the Navy. For one thing, it's given me a lot of confidence. For example, there was a fire at the fish and chip shop across the road from my dad's place the other day and people were running scared, but I didn't panic, because I knew I could control that situation.

If you want to take a gamble in life, I reckon you've got to do it before you're thirty, because you need to be settled down by thirty-five and have a steady career, an income and a good base. So this is my gamble: go outside for three years, maybe do GCSEs, go to university, settle down with someone. My ideal girl would be someone posh – with nothing dodgy about her, like going into town and stealing – you get a load of them like that around our area.

And if things don't go well and I end up skint, I can rejoin the Navy and go back to submarines, because I already know what that's all about.

LIEUTENANT COMMANDER DAN REISS, UNITED STATES NAVY

An American officer about to undertake the Perisher course, Lt Cdr Reiss spent time on board *Torbay* for experience.

The first time I went on a submarine as a midshipman, I was kind of like a kid in a candy store; I got to see things I'd only seen in a movie and then I realised very quickly that the movies are not even close. For example, they always make the control room look sleek and shiny, and sexy and huge, with people talking energetically to one another on the inter-radio. And none of it is like that.

The reality, I now know, is that you're on a vessel under-water, performing missions in a very difficult environment, both personally and politically, and it's dirty and smelly and you're exhausted. But sometimes, when you walk into the control room at night, and the crew's doing what it's supposed to be doing and doing it really well, you just look around and think, Damn, this is really cool . . .

When you're a submariner, whether you're a nuclear or marine engineer, or a warfare or operations officer, you cover everything there is to know. So I'm qualified to stand watch on a nuclear reactor plant or as an Officer of the Deck. The advantage of that is you have an absolutely critical understanding of what's happening across the entire ship at all times, so when something goes wrong, you know how it will impact everything else. If, say, a valve fails in the engine room, I know how that will affect the operational arm, and why, because of that, I couldn't launch a torpedo.

It was the small crew size which attracted me to submarines in the first place – I don't like to work with large groups of people. Also, I found that people aren't as focused on surface ships. On a submarine you have to focus almost continuously because there aren't enough guys to compensate for your lack of attention and also, if you don't, there's potential for getting hurt pretty badly. Being able to bring your mind into focus under extreme conditions – sleep deprivation, high stress and separation from your family – and still perform is very satisfying.

It's uncomfortable on board and it gets worse after about three days because the guys stop showering, so there's some nasty funk. You start to feel lethargic because of the lack of fresh air and then your sleep schedule gets out of whack. And when the effects of a six-hours on/six-hours off watch start to bite, you really feel it. Then there's the confinement; just being around people and bumping into them all of the time builds up over the first few days and guys get kind of angry with each other, and really grumpy and pissed-off about things. And then it'll slowly get better. Everyone goes: 'All right, I'm unhappy, I'm uncomfortable, but so is everyone else in this boat, so let's get over it.' And you settle into a routine and it actually becomes, I won't say peaceful, but a comfortable way to live, because you're on a schedule, you know your job and you trust all the other people around you.

Being on a boat with 120 other guys, you don't talk about your emotional needs too much. But I think you need another aspect of life, away from this place, to balance things out, so it's great to know you have family at home. But it's very hard on the families. The divorce rate is just incredible. It takes a very special person to be the spouse of a submariner, they really have a difficult life. My wife and I didn't get married until I was in active service, so we could see what the separation would be like, and we talked about it a lot, but even so, there's a lot to contend with. The isolation is incredible. It's not: 'Hey, I'll call you in a few weeks from wherever I am.' I've been on missions where you don't transmit at all for months at a time, and that's challenging for both of us. My wife has to take care of everything. Literally, the night before leaving to go to the UK, there was a massive storm and water flooded into our basement and kitchen, so we spent the night vacuuming up water and trying to deal with roof leaks. Then I flew out here and I got word from my wife that the roof has to be replaced. So a woman who is already struggling with two kids and a job now also has to go and find a contractor and the money to pay for the work within twenty-four hours of me leaving.

It's not just wives who are affected by lack of communication. I was on a mission when the 11 September attacks occurred, and the father of one of our sailors worked in the World Trade Centre. We got smatterings of messages through the official channels about what had happened, but it was a full month before he was able to find out that his dad was actually alive.

This is my first time on a British sub and the similarities are striking from a mechanical standpoint, so knowing where the equipment is and how things work is not the challenge, the real challenge is understanding the language barrier, and that's one of the reasons I'm here, to get over that hump. An exchange programme has been in place between the US Navy and the Royal Navy for fifty years now, where one American a year gets to go on the Perisher course, and that's me this year.

Also, the Royal Navy submarine force culture is different from the culture in the US submarine force. In the US Navy, we tend to be very focused on verbatim repeat-back of orders, very specific ways of executing procedures; you take your time, you move carefully and you don't move at all if there is any technical ambiguity, whereas in the Royal Navy there is much more of an inherent trust of the professionalism of the engineering guys, and that difference results in a little bit more freedom of action in the forward department.

Whichever side of the pond you are, the captain is critically important. I've been under captains who've almost killed us because of their actions or their failure to act properly, and I've had captains who have almost killed us emotionally because they're so berating. But then there are those at the opposite extremes. I can think of one captain I've served under who was so inspiring that if he said to me, 'I need you to go to sea tomorrow,' I would drop everything and go to him. You get highs and lows on a sub, but they're all driven by one man, who sets the tone for the entire boat.

The most important thing on a submarine is how you react under pressure. You need to know a guy is going to take appropriate action when bad things are happening, and that he'll do it quickly and without regard to his personal safety. If you get a fire on board, the submarine will fill with smoke and noxious fumes within seconds, and if a guy isn't able to respond immediately and take action, we could all die. But the really crucial thing for me is that a guy's got to be honest, not just in terms of telling the truth, he's got to be honest about himself, about the condition he's in, his strengths and capabilities, but also where his weaknesses lie.

Weakness isn't tolerated in any submarine in any way, shape or form. So if the guys see that you're mentally weak or easily perturbed in some way, they'll just goad you a bit to see if it's a personality trait or just a little quirk. If it's a real fault in your personality, it's most likely you won't stay in the submarine service very long. It's kind of a self-regulating organisation in that way.

PETTY OFFICER ENGINEERING TECHNICIAN (MESM) CARL RELPH

Working in the engine room upper level, PO Relph is a respected member of the marine engineering department.

I'm originally from Whitehaven on the west coast of Cumbria. My mum was a trainee nurse and my dad was a doctor; they played doctors and nurses, and that's how I appeared. But Dad then left us, and Mum decided we'd go and live with her parents, so, growing up, I was strongly influenced by my grandparents. Grandma's the religious one, she's always praying for me, and Granddad took on the father-figure role and taught me the basic things to get through life – honesty, respect, treating people as you want to be treated yourself. In other words, all the old-fashioned rules, as they're classed these days.

SUB

Coming from a single-parent family, I have always been very close to Mum; we've got a kind of brother–sister relationship, the sort where I can go to her about anything. She's always been very honest with me about Dad, she told me all about him, and showed me pictures of him. She also said that if I ever wanted to find him then I should, although I haven't, and I'm happy with that. I'd like to have met him earlier in my life, but if he turned up on my doorstep now, I'd probably give him a size ten up his you-know-what. He hasn't bothered for twenty-nine years, so why bother now? Mum's since got married to someone else and, luckily, I get on really well with her husband.

I joined the Navy when I was sixteen, and I'm now an engineer and work in the engine room on the upper level where we've got the main equipment, including the turbo-generators, which produce electricity, the engines which keep the submarine and all our sonar stuff cool, and the air compressors, which ensure we've got air and propulsion, which is the movement of the submarine backwards and forwards. I love this room because you've got two types of watch-keeping. The first is the electrical watch-keeping, which happens in a room where you've got four or five people. And the second is the mechanical watch-keeping, which is out on the platform itself. There's no doubt that by being with machines so much you end up humanising them, especially if you're sat there trying to get one of them to work. I'll often shout: 'Come on, girl!'

My job is great in as much as I haven't got anyone constantly sat on my shoulder watching my every move; I can just go out with my torch, do my rounds and make sure everything is as it should be. For me, one of the best bits of the job is working in the distilling plant where we have the Brabies, which are the distilling machines that produce all our drinking water. To start them off, you basically take seawater, boil it and it then evaporates, leaving the salt behind. The vapour is then channelled into a cooling tube where it is cooled off, forming water again, which is purified.

There is a chain of command on board and everything works through a divisional system. In the engine room I've got just one person above me and that's my section head, called Chief Parfitt. He does his own thing, but if there's anything immediate I need to attend to, say if I had court tomorrow or needed time off for something, then I go and see him. There's also Mark Alder, the marine engineer and officer (MEO). He's the top boss, which means that anything important we do must go through him, although he has certain delegates, like Lieutenant Forrester, who is my divisional officer, and if I've got any problems, family-wise, money-wise, anything like that, then I'd see him.

I think the hardest thing you find with a submarine is

the initial going away, because you're tearing yourself away from your family life. It's especially difficult if you've got a new girlfriend because they don't actually realise what that entails. With me, I start shutting down, usually about a week, maybe ten days before I go to sea, and I just try and turn my feelings in, put the blinkers on. If a lot of people working on submarines knew how much they'd miss their families, I don't think they'd ever go away to sea.

I kind of have a girlfriend but, I don't know, things are a bit bad at the moment. We got together when I was doing a degree, which meant I was on a shore establishment all the time, so she basically got used to me coming home every night. But now I'm back to a seaborne submarine, the routine's completely changed, and she's finding it difficult to cope with. While I don't have any children myself, she's got a four-year-old girl who I've brought up since she was nine months old, so I see her as my daughter now, and I'd find leaving her very hard. My girlfriend and I have regular conversations, but I don't know what's going to happen. Ideally, I'd like to work through it all, but at the end of the day, if she's unhappy, I'm not going to press-gang her into staying in a relationship she doesn't want to be in.

The thing is everybody makes sea time what it is. Once you're on your submarine and away it's great, because there's always something to keep you from sitting down and contemplating all this kind of stuff. If we all sat around and mooned about, then it would be a really horrible place to be. But a lot of the guys on board are fantastic. I've got a couple of people who I'll talk to if I'm really feeling the strain, and quite often they'll just make a joke about things, which is good. Likewise, you've got idiots who'll take the mick, have a laugh and some banter, and it's a good pick-me-up.

In the past, my way of dealing with problems was to go out for the night and drink myself into oblivion. I suppose I was quite an angry individual back then. I got myself into quite a bit of trouble – not doing what I was told to, getting into brawls and fights, all that kind of thing. I'd start by getting into a slanging match with someone, they'd take a pop, and I'd end up punching their head in. Consequently, I'd end up getting into trouble back on the submarine, maybe fined or something. Looking back, I think my behaviour was to do with coming from a small town and moving to a big city like Plymouth, where I was trying to make my mark.

To be honest, I've grown up a lot; now I'd rather play a game of rugby than get into a fight. In fact, I now play for the Navy in Rugby League and for local teams in Rugby Union. But don't get me wrong, I still like to have a good blow-out every now and again, and be the life and soul of the party; I just don't go as mad as I used to.

With my own career, I'm trying to progress as quickly as I can now. So, more than anything, I want to keep my head down, study hard and qualify in all the positions I can. That way, I hope, I'll eventually move up through the ranks.

PETTY OFFICER (COMMUNICATIONS INFORMATION SYSTEMS) ANDY 'ROBBIE' ROBINSON

A senior communications rating, PO Robinson is responsible for providing guidance to Command on all communications-related issues.

I'm one of the planesmen, and I'm also the radio supervisor on board, in charge of all external communications.

I think being a communicator is probably one of the hardest jobs to do. If we're away on patrol for three months or so, we can't transmit to the outside world, although we can receive incoming stuff, and I'm actually the only person on board who can decrypt these signals. I've had several occasions where people on board have family who have become really ill or died, and that news gets fed to me, and I've then got to tell the Command that AB Whoever's mum or dad has just died.

I might then go down to lunch or breakfast and see that bloke, and he'll be saying: 'I'm going to see my dad or my gran when I get back ... ' and I'm thinking, No, you're not, you poor sod. But you can't tell him when you're on the boat, because he could throw a wobbly, which would threaten all our safety, and you can't tell anyone else, because there'll be Chinese whispers. I'm also one of the first people to hear about programme changes. Sometimes I'll know we're going to be extended a further month or more at sea, when everyone's expecting to get home in a couple of days' time, and I've got to keep quiet about that as well.

Planes has got to be the worst job on board; it's a nightmare. When you come up to PD [periscope depth], it can be really rough and you're bouncing around, so you have to try and keep the boat on depth and on course, and you've got so many back-seat drivers idly standing around you in the control room – who of course all know exactly what to do – even though they've never actually done it themselves.

The main reason for coming up to periscope depth is to signal the outside world that, yes, we are still alive and kicking. All our communications go directly into the UK SUBCAMS (Submarine Broadcast Control and Monitoring

Station): we're looked after by Commander Task Force 311 or CTF 345, who are the admirals up at Northwood, and they feed all signal traffic from shoreside into our system, which we generate in the WT, weapons training, shack, and distribute to the Command, who then filters it down.

I have a very good relationship with the commander, which is just as well, because the WT shack is right next door to his cabin, so he hears everything that goes on. Sometimes, if we're a bit pissed off about what's going on below decks, we speak a little bit louder to make sure he hears stuff. But this commander is absolutely brilliant; you can knock on his door anytime and sit down and have a chat.

I left school with hardly any qualifications whatsoever because I just didn't like it, and used to mess around all the time. I don't know why. But I have kids of twenty and twenty-one and they're both at university, so they're going down the brainy track. I'm proud of them, although they sponge off me all the time, it's, 'Dad I want £50 for *this*, I want £100 for *that* . . . ' But I don't mind, because when I was younger I didn't really get much off my parents. Maybe it's completely wrong, but all I want is for them to know that if they are ever stuck, I'm there for them.

I split up with my first wife and without a doubt my divorce was due to the life I was leading; I hardly saw my kids grow up because I was away at sea, and then later on

my wife got herself a job, and she progressed and progressed, and I sometimes thought she was looking down on
me and thinking, He's only a petty officer in the Navy,
that's not good enough for me. But she wasn't. I remember coming back home from the sub and my wife said to
me, 'I want a divorce.' I was pissed off at the time, but I
now get on with my ex-wife, so I've got no problems
there, and it was probably one of the best birthday presents
she has ever given me, because I met Maria.

We had gone up to Tromsø, Norway, which is a really
beautiful part of the world. One of my mates rang me and
said: 'I'm talking to some gorgeous girl. I think you'd better
get your arse round here.' So I met Maria, and we just
clicked. The boat sailed from Tromsø, but I managed to get
an extra shore leave, and we spent a few days together and
it just went from there.

Because of the divorce I didn't have a penny to scratch
my arse with and Maria knew that, but we've got our own
house now and enough money to get us through, so I'm
laughing. About two years ago, Maria moved across to the
UK, found herself a job and we got married in January this
year, and life's looking rosy. We're off to Naples in June as
a foreign draft, and I'm really looking forward to that. I'm
going to meet a whole bunch of new people out there and
work on my suntan, because we obviously don't see any
sun on the sub whatsoever.

Don't tell the lads down in the hatch about all this happiness – they think I'm a miserable git because I moan about everything. But that's just my aura. Secretly, I'm a happy guy. And I love the camaraderie between everyone onboard a submarine, I just love being able to talk crap, swear as much as you want and be as un-PC as possible.

When we are at sea, and fast and deep, you just miss things. I miss a good comfortable bed, I miss fresh air, I miss being able to pop down the shops or go for a couple of beers on a Friday night, but mainly I just miss the company of my wife, and her cooking.

The food on board can be bland, although I accept the fact that they have got 120 people to cater for, which isn't easy. But I'm probably spoiled because my wife is such a good cook. Being Norwegian, she loves her whale, and on Friday night at home she makes wonderful whale-meat steak and chips. Whale is a little bit salty, with no fat in it whatsoever and it has a wonderful taste.

LIEUTENANT MARCUS ROSE

Deputy Weapons Engineering Officer

Lt Rose deputises for the weapons engineering office (WEO) and, like Mike Greaves (pages 143–8), he is the other fire-control officer.

I'm a weapons engineer but I also do things like ship control, officer of the watch and periscope watch-keeping. Ship control is the guy sat behind the planesman and the power watch-keeper in the control room. Basically you are in charge of controlling the trim and the body weight of the submarine, all the high-pressure systems and looking after the planesman, making sure he's on depth and on the right course.

The planesman has got the stick in front of him and so he controls the control surfaces, the afterplanes and the foreplanes, which keep our depth, and also the rudder, which is used to keep course.

It's not easy, because you not only have to look at the course and the depth, you also look at the pitch of the submarine. You might be on depth at the moment, but if you've got a two- or three-degree angle up on the boat, you can very quickly come off depth, because it's like a plane, it will fly its way up. The responsiveness of the submarine depends on speed. If you're going fast then it's very, very responsive, so much so that some of the planesmen are only qualified up to a certain speed. You only need a very small amount of angle on the boat and if you were going at twenty-odd knots you would just fly out of control.

We have four ballast tanks outside the pressure hull, two forward and two aft, which, when on the surface, we fill with air to keep us buoyant. When the submarine dives, we open the vents, which allows all the air out of the ballast tanks. They then fill with water, which makes us heavy and causes us to dive. Once we have dived, we alter the weight of the submarine using internal compensating tanks.

The number of people in the control room depends on what we're doing. If we're deep, then you'll have an officer of the watch, someone on electronic charts, a ship controller, a panel watch-keeper and a planesman. You'll always have at least one or two on ops on the command system, someone on forward staff who is a junior rate, who does all the ventilation-system changes, and then there are always three or four in the sound room.

You get busier if you are up at PD, because you will then have a periscope watch-keeper in there, a hoist operator, who puts the mast up and down, and extra people close up on the charts: one just doing the charts and one doing all the logs. And then if you are surfacing it gets even more busy because you've got all the bridge team up there and all the equipment coming through as well.

When we go to PD someone has to be on the periscope at all times and you do something called 'continuous all-round look', where you are constantly going round in circles. You have two handles on the periscope: one controls the torque of the motor that drives the periscope and the other controls the elevation of what you are looking at.

Looking out of a periscope is a bit surreal because you are actually underwater but what you are seeing makes you feel you've got your head out of the water. I enjoy it because it's one of the few instances you get to see what's going on in the outside world. You can see quite a lot of marine life up there, whales and dolphins, and you see a lot of dhows out in the Gulf. During the day we do twenty minutes on, twenty minutes off for three hours. Overnight you drop that to fifteen minutes at a time because it's a lot more stressful at night; also, you're behind curtains, because you don't want to lose your night vision from all the lights in the control room, and you get very warm, which makes it very tiring.

SUB

This morning I was on the periscope; it was quite a nice morning, and there was a warship out there, *Sutherland* I think it was, which is a Type 23, and a couple of fishing vessels as well.

I really do enjoy the life. If you work hard it's quite satisfying, and it's very close knit, and you make really good friends, which is probably the biggest plus.

I've got a girlfriend, who I shall be engaged to, hopefully, when I get back. Genevieve, her name is. She lives in Plymouth and she's a nurse. I haven't proposed yet, but I bought a ring up in Glasgow with Mike, who came with me as a sanity check. I don't really understand what the carats are, and what's better, platinum or gold, and he does as he's been married for years. Anyway, we bought it and I've got it in a locker in the accommodation space at the moment.

Genevieve is the daughter of an ex-sailor who was a doctor in the Navy, and probably because her dad did it, she is very good at putting up with me being away. Five years we've been together, so it's been a while, but I'm due off the submarine very soon and I would very much like her to move to London, because that's where I'm supposed to be going next to do a missile job up there.

It's such a big thing, isn't it? Not something you want to do lightly. I'm slightly concerned she will say 'no'. But she likes the Navy uniform, so I'll stick on my number ones and take her out to dinner, probably Tanners in Plymouth, and propose to her that night. I've told Ben and Phil, who are my mates on the submarine. I think they might come out with us, along with their other halves, if it goes well, or I may just go out with them if it goes badly.

GENEVIEVE HOLT, FIANCÉE
OF MARCUS ROSE

Genevieve is a nurse who lives in Plymouth. She is engaged to Lieutenant Marcus Rose.

I met Marcus in a nightclub; he looked very smart in his chinos and shirt, his sleeves were rolled up, and he had nice arms, very hairy, and I remember thinking he was quite a manly man.

I was quite shocked to find out he was in the Navy because I swore I wouldn't go down that path. I'd been brought up in a naval family; my father was a doctor in the Navy. I remember once commenting to my mum that I saw my teachers more often than my dad, and she got quite upset about it, but that was just a fact. So I knew about the Navy . . .

Anyway, Marcus and I shared a taxi back and swapped numbers, and then he went off to Torbay and we didn't actually meet again until January because of his timescales and me working shifts as a nurse, and that had to be for breakfast.

Valentine's Day was our first proper date, where we actually had time to go out for a meal and talk.

He had booked a restaurant which he told me was a steak restaurant, and they said, 'Oh, we're a fish restaurant,' and I remember Marcus saying mournfully, 'But I don't like fish.' Anyway, we shared a fish pie, very tasty, but maybe not the Valentine's Day I had hoped for. It would have been nice if he had chosen somewhere a bit more romantic.

Then he went to sea for four months and we still hadn't had a chance to get to know each other, but we knew there was a link and that we wanted to keep seeing each other.

One thing I did know was that he didn't stop talking about submarines – you could really see he had a passion for it. One time I went to Devil's Point in Plymouth and watched his boat come in, and I remember being hugely proud of him; to be honest, it's difficult not to get emotional because they've gone away and done something worthwhile and positive for the country – which sounds a bit cheesy – but it's the case, really. The sad thing is for security reasons I'll never know the full extent of what they've done or where they've gone, but I know they've worked so hard and I don't think people really appreciate what they do. He always looks extremely pasty and skinny when he comes off the boat, not particularly healthy, to be honest.

It's very emotional when they come back, not just because of the excitement you're going to see them, but there's the nervousness because you haven't seen them in so long and you hope you still feel the same way about each other.

At first it is great fun. You stock the fridge with all the delicious things you know they love and we go out to the cinema, and out for dinner, and you even buy new clothes because you want to look nice because you haven't seen him for a while, and it's the honeymoon period all over again. And I guess in a sense they do expect to be spoilt a bit, you know, 'I've been away for five months, the last thing I want to do is a DIY job.' Nor does he want to hear about any problems and you haven't emailed about those anyway, because what can he do about them? He can't ring me and he can't get off the submarine.

There's a number of things that have happened in the last two years that I've maybe not been totally honest about with Marcus in an email because I don't want to distress him, or I don't know how he's going to react to them.

The most obvious issue would be my mother, who was diagnosed with cancer. He missed all the doctors' appointments, the chemotherapy trips, the scans, the scan results.

He'd email and ask how things had gone and if they've gone well, but the last thing I was going to do was say, 'Well, actually, Marcus, it's really bad news.' Even my mother dying . . . I couldn't email him that news.

My mother died three weeks ago. Marcus didn't ring me until the Monday, and that was probably the longest four days ever. And by the time he rang, everything had calmed down, the crying had stopped, a bit of acceptance had set in so he didn't see my emotion, and I don't know if he fully understands the journey I've been through.

I was very lucky, the Navy did everything they could to help me. I think they appreciated the fact that I'm twenty-three and my mother was young, too, and that this shouldn't really have happened. As it turned out, the boat had to return to Plymouth and the minute they got along-side, Marcus was allowed off and he came to the funeral on Friday – and then joined the boat again on Saturday.

Marcus has got a habit of bringing back the most bizarre presents: odd socks, some strange bright-orange and blue candles in this hideous fake crystal cup, and a tartan miniskirt, to name a few, and for our second Valentine's Day, he decided I should have gerbils, and now I have these two lovely gerbils called Splodger and Valerie. Obviously, I knew I'd be the one looking after them.

Anyway, last time he came home, as soon as he walked through the door he handed me a bottle of champagne, and he's never bought a bottle of champagne for me in his life, and then he said, 'Oh, here's your other present,' and he pulled out a box and got down on one knee . . .

My mother never got the chance to know Marcus properly because he was constantly away. I asked him during his last lot of leave if we could go away as a family, and we all went to France for a few days. He did say he was glad we did because he started to get to know my mum. He had no idea she spoke fluent French, for instance, and was amazed when she started speaking it. I don't think he really appreciated what she had to offer. Anyway, I'm so glad we had that chance. I remember Marcus saying goodbye to my mum, they were hugging in the doorway, and I just took this mental picture because I had this feeling that was it.

I haven't had that many dramas in my life – it's only the last year when I've really needed him – but you can't help who you fall in love with. He's a lovely guy, he treats me really well, but he goes to sea for four months at a time and you can't bin someone because of that. If all I've got to do is cope on my own for four months, it's not the end of the world, and your mother can only die once.

We've had some fantastic times, too, that I have not mentioned. I guess the point is, despite there being some very hard and distressing times, we are incredibly lucky. It would be very easy to blame the Navy for all the times I have had to handle life's dramas on my own, but Marcus has a job he loves and that he's good at, and I am so proud of that. His time away also gives me the opportunity to focus on aspects of my life and I have achieved things that some women may not get the chance or opportunity to do in a 'normal' relationship.

It's sad, but there's not a great deal of support among my civilian friends regarding the fact that I'm on my own so often, doing nothing with my evenings. It would be quite nice to go out for dinner once in a while. But they don't say, 'Oh, you must come over for dinner when Marcus is away,' it's always, 'We must meet up when Marcus is back.' Maybe they don't appreciate I'm alone for so long.

Marcus goes to sea, we miss each other, but we remember what we love about each other, then when he comes home we do all the fun things you do in a new relationship, like dinners out, the cinema and buying gifts for each other, and by the time he is driving me mad and getting under my feet, he goes back to sea for a few months. I will no doubt have a totally different attitude as life becomes more complicated with age and throws more problems our way, but I guess, in the words of my mother whenever I moaned to her, 'That's life in a blue suit.'

WILMOT SMITH, CONTRACTOR

Smith was on board temporarily, teaching staff to operate the new mainframe sonar system, made by the company he works for, when the boat set sail – with him on board.

It's mostly bad luck I'm here. I work for the company that built the mainframe sonar on this platform, and I got chosen to come and support the trials. Because I'm from an operational background, they thought I would have a better understanding of what's going on. Actually, I was a submariner for fourteen years before I left the Service, about eight years ago.

It's strange, because I did get quite nervous coming on board. I'd forgotten so many of the delights: the vertical ladders, which now I've put on weight I find very difficult to negotiate, the cramped corridors, the low ceilings and jutting valves that catch you on the top of your head. When I was a submariner none of that used to bother me whatsoever, but I realise I have got used to living in civvy street. Also, I think another problem is when you are not actually a member of the ship's company, you are slightly alien, and that bothers me quite a bit, the fact that I was once a part of the crew and now when I come on board I'm an outsider.

The cramped sleeping conditions bother me too, I'm sleeping in the Bomb Shop, and I'm extremely tired at the minute, because I've not managed to achieve much sleep with all the comings and goings of the weapons crew, twenty-four-seven.

But the worst thing of all, the single thing that drives me crazy, is that there's nowhere whatsoever you can go to find personal space to have a quick five minutes on your own.

I would never go back to this. Coming back on board as a civilian makes me wonder, how the hell did I put up with all this? It's so cramped. You get used to sleeping in a nice big bed – or just simply being able to sit up in bed. And listening to music.

My job's done, so the earliest I can get off the better, to be honest, although who knows when that will be.

It's been five days so far and I really miss my family. I miss walking my dog in the fresh air. I'm constantly thinking of them all, and then I think, Oh God, when can I get off this thing? But, in a way, this separation has been good,

I think I'll appreciate my home and my family more when I go back.

The first thing I'm going to do when I get home is get into my shower and stay in it for about twenty minutes, which you certainly can't do on board, as they have to preserve water.

The second thing will be to get my clothes in the washing machine. You stink when you get back. You, and all your clothes will have the submarine aroma, which is bad, bad, bad, although you don't notice it at sea, because we all smell the same on board.

Then I think it will be straight to bed, my nice, big bed . . .

LIEUTENANT CRAIG SPACEY
Deputy Marine Engineer Officer

Among other duties, Lt Spacey is responsible for the maintenance and operation of propulsion, power plant, distribution and fresh water production systems. He also exercises the ship's company in damage control and fire-fighting, ensuring that all are regularly put through their paces.

These submarines are very good boats, but they are getting to an age now where a lot of what we call class defects are starting to crop up, but the reactor, which is what all the money is spent on, is very good quality gear.

There has to be an inspection of the reactor after shutting down, but we have to wait for the radiation levels to dissipate enough to make our entry, and also see how hot it is in the reactor compartment, which depends on your running, i.e. how fast you've been going. If we've steamed in from the other side of the Atlantic, so we've been in a full-power state for quite a long time, it will be very hot. On average, we have to wait about eighteen hours before we go in.

I then put on set of white overalls, a white skullcap, little white booties that go over my shoes, and two sets of gloves, which is standard entry-wear to protect you because there will be potential for contamination in quite high levels in the reactor compartment, which is why we don't go in there at sea. It's all monitored; a guy with a Geiger counter sweeps you before you go in, and again after you come out, and checks you're not contaminated, and 99.999 times you won't have anything on you.

Nuclear power has a bad rap because a lot of people don't understand the genuine benefits, and also how it's regulated and managed to the point where you have a crew like us who are all happy to work, live and sleep very close to a nuclear reactor. There are issues with waste, and we do generate nuclear waste, so at some point we have to discharge relatively small amounts of primary coolant into the sea. Primary coolant is water. It's the same colour as water, it's not green, it doesn't glow, if you saw it sat in a beaker, it looks just like a beaker of water, except it has a big radiation sticker stuck on it. But we don't discharge within twelve miles of land, or known fishing grounds, and we do it in open ocean, and generally at depth.

There are plenty of real dangers on board. A fire on a sub is very serious, because you are in an enclosed atmosphere. A few years ago HMS *Tireless* had an explosion on the forward escape, which put the atmosphere out of specification in less than thirty seconds, and the debris and smoke that was generated meant you couldn't see in many of the compartments. So that's why we quite rigorously test our ship's company with fire drills, and expect that in the event of something happening, everyone's actions would be instinctive.

When we fight an incident we use what we call 'continuous aggressive attack', no matter how small. You think where a fire is going to start – it will be in a bin, or the chip pan might catch fire in the galley – and if you respond correctly that should be very easy to put out.

If there is a big fire, we very quickly have two guys turn up with breathing apparatus sets on. At the same time we call up a fearnought team, a three-man fire-fighting team in fear-naught suits, to go and attack the scene of the fire and, at the same time, we will be preparing another team to relieve that team, in case they get beaten back because it's too hot or their extinguishers have run out. A damage control headquarters sets up in the wardroom, and all of that decision-making is run by the captain, advised by the damage-control team.

There's a lot to think about because, you have to remember, all this might be happening while we are doing something we haven't told another nation we are doing, and we don't want them to know we are there, so we can't surface. On the other hand, we may have such a serious fire we would want someone to assist our submarine, but we can't communicate because of where we are . . .

Trafalgar-class submarines have to be very flexible in their tasking, because of the small number we have got, and the commitments being placed on the submarine service at the minute, which are considerable. As soon as the submarine sails, the programme will change; the programme changes hourly sometimes, regarding what you will be doing, where you will be going, and why. The T-class are primarily there to protect our Trident boats, the boats with nuclear missiles, so that's what we will be sent out to protect first, and that could happen any time or place. But, if anything emergent happens, for instance, another nation's submarine being where it shouldn't, there's also the reactive tasking, which this submarine is set up for, and we might go have a look, or maybe fend them off.

As soon as the captain knows we are about to get sent on an emergent tasking, before he even tells us what's about to happen, he will cut all submarine communications straight away. So your family won't know your schedule is about to change until they are eventually informed by Fleet Devonport, who will just tell them there is a major tasking and they don't know when we will be back.

We had one situation where we were literally right at the end of our deployment and then got sent away for another eight weeks on top, which obviously had massive implications for our families. I had a two-week holiday booked, and my wife had booked off work, and she is a nurse, so can only have a certain amount of time off. So she had two weeks' holiday sat on her own.

My wife is happy when she thinks she knows the set time I am going to be back. But when suddenly someone's saying we are not going to be back for another eight weeks, that gets her upset. She is now at the point where she doesn't believe anything I tell her. But actually, she's quite right, because she can't plan her life with certainty, and it's probably best she doesn't believe what I or anyone says, because then her hopes aren't raised.

Food becomes an issue in that extra time at sea. We always maintain a certain level of food on board, because we know we might be tasked to do these things, but effectively you get put on the Atkins Diet and you are fed tins of meat, not very much carbs, and certainly no fresh food. I lost over a stone and a half in those eight weeks. My mum and my wife were going, 'Oh God, we want to go on a submarine, you lose so much weight.' It's not very nice, though. For instance, we ended up with one slice of bread per man, per day. You wrap your bread in a cellophane wrapper and put it in the fridge, and then all day you're thinking, Shall I have that slice for breakfast or lunch? Maybe I'll have it at lunch with my soup. No, I might keep it for the evening . . .

Also, normally, we engineers take a lot of nutty to sea with us, because we have a tradition back aft where we have a lot of tea and biscuits, which we like to share; it's quite a nice thing to do. But suddenly you have two packets of biscuits and a pack of wine gums and Maltesers to last you eight weeks.

The thing is though, we expect our submarine to get sent away, and although for a day or so after it happens people are gloomy because they thought they were going home, you then just get stuck into it because that's your job. And, actually, those operations are very interesting. There's privileged information people on board a submarine get to see and witness, which they can't tell anyone about, and the only other people on the planet who know as well are a small group of people from Northwood who are directing the submarine, and the Cabinet and the Prime Minister, because he has personally directed our submarine to do that tasking. So it makes you feel quite privileged when you are doing operations like that.

People accept being away on a submarine; it's when the programme continually changes and there is a perception on board that it's because of bad planning that people get upset. For instance, when the submarine goes east of Suez, which we are doing all the time now, nine times out of ten you get stuck out there for longer. Why haven't we been relieved by another submarine? Either the submarine that's relieving you has a problem and it can't come out and relieve you on time, or you've got a problem and can't go and relieve the other people on time. It's neither submarine's fault, it's the stresses and strains of having an ageing submarine fleet, and government after government who never fund the armed forces, and who don't want to fund them until there's a war, by which time it's too late. That's what we live with.

PETTY OFFICER CATERER
TOMMY TUCKER

As head of the catering team, PO Tucker is responsible for ordering and storing supplies to produce a varied menu, managing the galley and ensuring food hygiene. He is also a planesman.

I am the PO caterer, so I basically run the menus and look after everyone's diet and health while we are away at sea.

I did four years as a civilian chef before I even joined up. I had a good job cheffing in the restaurant I worked at, but I just fancied a change. And then I joined the Navy and learnt a hell of a lot more than I had when I was in civilian street. I run everything to do with dietary requirements: looking after vegetarians, anyone who has allergy problems; all that has to come into my head when I am writing menus or ordering in the food for when we go to sea.

It's a terribly difficult job. There's not many people I know who could do this – there's so much abuse and criticism. The food is always the first thing that gets picked on, shouted at, argued about – you have to have a big set of shoulders to do my job on a submarine. The submariner's life can be a bit depressing and if we don't produce great food then the ship's company's morale goes further and further down, and it just gets really messy then.

So it's my job to produce stuff to bring morale back up, get everybody happy during the day with chocolate bars and nice cakes and that sort of stuff. When the captain knows he's about to dish out some bad news – say we are going to disappear for a couple of weeks on top of when we were scheduled to return home – everyone will be complaining and it's down to me to try and get everybody's spirits back up. OK, we are not going back home, but there's brilliant food on tonight ... Things like black on black – chocolate sponge cake with chocolate sauce is a great favourite – and a good morale-booster; it's very sickly and sweet but the lads love it, so that's what I save for, when we disappear.

Obviously there are the 'nutty buckets' as well or the 'happy bucket', some call it. The bucket gets left somewhere prominent, you walk over, sign your name and select the choc bar of your choice. We sell everything from wine gums to mint humbugs, plus chocolate bars galore, Snickers, Mars, Caramacs, Crunchies, Maltesers, Minstrels – you name it.

Before we sail, I order fresh, frozen and dry food, and then on three separate days between twenty and thirty-five pallets of food will turn up, depending on where we're going and how long we are going for, but it's two full arctic trucks with six-foot high pallets all marked up. You need quite a lot of food for 120 blokes. From an empty store-room to filling up is around £40,000.

We use the weapons embarkation hatch to load everything. We store the dried first, then we do the frozen and then finally the fresh a couple of days later, once we have cleaned down. At this stage we have got a basic catalogue, which is all your cold meats, your chicken, your pork and beef – we take four different types, beef fillet, beef strip loin, beef rump and minced beef – then you have your sausage and bacon. Every Saturday me and my co-chef sit down and write the menu and I give it to the logistics officer, he checks it to make sure all the spelling is correct, then he gives it to the captain and if he's happy with it, we go for it.

Lunch today was cottage pie, gravy, mashed potato and peas, or a nice big ploughman's salad. Dinner tonight is homemade chicken and mushroom pie, or lamb stew with dumplings and apple pie and custard. The menus are quite set and routine when we go to sea, which is traditional in the Royal Navy for every boat, submarines and skimmers. For example, Wednesday night is always curry night and we shall have two choices of curry, with naan breads, poppadoms and all that sort of stuff. Thursday is always a baked spud choice, so you get a baked potato with either train smash, which is chopped-up leftover breakfast baked beans, or leftover curry and chilli. Friday, without fail, is fish and chips: deep-fried cod, chips and mushy peas. Saturday is steak night, Sunday is a big hearty roast and Sunday night is always pizza with chips and beans for your evening meal.

We also do a one o'clock in the morning soup, which is made out of everything that is left over from dinner, so your veg, baked potatoes, chicken and mushroom pie, which all get blitzed up and made into a big broth, and you have that when you're feeling peckish at one o'clock in the morning with a bread roll.

I have some knowledge regarding proteins and starches, and so we tend not to put potatoes on with rice and pasta, because you are going to be doubling up on the starch in your system, and we try and get lots of greens and vegetables and salad stuff down people, although they then tend to pour mayonnaise all over it, which sort of defeats the object. After two weeks we'll be running out of fresh food, but we will make rice salads and pasta salads and coleslaw. We try to make the menu people actually enjoy eating, so a lot of the time we go for council-house food, as we call it, like a cheesy ham eggy, also known as a wham-bam, which is minced ham and cheese on a piece of toast, with a fried egg on top.

I do have to think about nutrition: are they going to get fat eating this? Obviously it is a little bit difficult to stay slim on a submarine because you could have three big, hearty meals a day. Not everybody eats all the meals, because if you were to sit and eat every single meal we produce, you would go home about six or seven stone heavier than when you turned up, particularly as exercise is difficult on a boat; there is only one bike and one rower between 120 blokes.

It's not as though anyone is getting anything different, but the officers do get to pick what they want out of the two choices for dinner. They actually get asked every morning what they would like for dinner and then my chefs provide that many numbers – because we always say, don't bite the hand that feeds you – they are our bosses, they do our reports, they give us our promotions, so the officers are the most important people on the submarine.

I got married three weeks ago. Because *Torbay* is running quite a lot, we tend to be away quite a lot of the time, which does put a bit of strain on our relationship, although she knew I was in the Armed Forces when we met.

Luckily, I hadn't been away for about a year before, so we had spent practically every day together. But then I went away for seven months and then saw her for four days, and then another seven months away, and I came back and saw her for about two months, and in that time we moved house, got married and went on honeymoon to Las Vegas for a week.

Because I had been away a lot, I had a lot of money in the bank, so we decided to spend it all on a Las Vegas honeymoon, which was really, really good fun. We did everything we could: Cirque de Soleil, shows up and down the Strip, and we went into every single hotel and casino you could go into.

But then I got a phone call giving me three days' notice to come back to Scotland, which was ten days earlier than I should have been coming back. That didn't go down too well; the wife got a bit upset about that, but I think she was more upset that we had only spent one night together at our new house, and I was leaving. But she knows the score; it's what I do for a living, it's the Navy – a life in a blue suit, as they call it.

I left some flowers on the sideboard with a card because it is her birthday in about ten days – and I won't be back for that, either . . .

But I can't knock the job; the money's great and sometimes it's brilliant on board. You can't ask for more than that. It's just with the Navy, you can't ever really plan your life, although I am hoping we will be home for a month so I can spend some time with my wife before we get away again. We don't spend enough time together as it is, so the more time we get the better, because I really love my wife, she's brilliant, I wouldn't swap her for the world.

LEADING ENGINEERING TECHNICIAN (MESM) DAN WEBSTER

LET Webster is a member of the marine engineering department and is a fire-control technician.

My entire family has been in the Navy, apart from my mum – but there's still time! They were all skimmers, surface fleet, but I wanted to do something different, so I went for submarines. My missus wasn't very happy, but she didn't really get a lot of say. My little brother was doing basic training at the same time as me, and he decided to do the same thing, so we've ended up with two submariners in the family.

I'm a fire-control maintainer; I fire the Spearfish torpedoes – massive great things – and the TLAM weapons. Sonar will build up a tactical picture. I'll choose and select the target using my software, then just attack it.

SUB

My wife, Julie, doesn't like me being away, but she copes. The money and job security keeps me here because there's not a lot of either of those outside. But it was horrible leaving the twins, I found it really difficult this time. We've been trying for a baby for ten years and we finally got there after the third shot at IVF. We had twins just before Christmas, Rhys and Alanna.

It was a very strange process. You're putting your personal life on the table for everybody to see and you have all these tests, and they delve into your background. And the questions they ask! Me and my wife were in with the doctor and she asked how many previous partners I'd had, plus, for good measure she threw in: 'Have you ever cheated on your wife?' You don't really want to be discussing those things with your wife sat next to you, do you? She's there! I'm not likely to say anything, am I?

But the worst part was when the first two attempts failed. My missus was in tears most of the time. We paid a bit more money for the extra fertility treatment the last time; we went for assisted hatching. She had to do a pregnancy test after two weeks and I was there when she did it, and it came back positive. You then have to go for a scan two weeks later, and this time there were two strong heartbeats. I was over the moon, but very apprehensive, as it had already failed twice. The next twelve weeks were the worst, because you can fail at any point, but once you're past that, it gets more exciting.

Julie had to have a caesarean because one of the twins didn't turn. The birth was a bit clinical. 'Be here at half-seven and you are going in at nine o' clock.' But I wouldn't have missed it for the world; it was brilliant. When the babies came out, I couldn't see everything, because there was a big screen up, all I could see was the wife's head, and when I heard the first one come out and start crying, well, it all got a bit foggy for me ... The little girl came out first, and then I was saying, to myself, 'Better be a boy, better be a boy ...' And it was a little boy! Brilliant. Amazing. They were so alike when they were born, they had to give the girl a little pink tag, and the boy a blue one because we didn't know which one was which.

Julie was in hospital for four days, then I stayed home for another six weeks to help her while she recovered. I always said I wouldn't do dirty nappies but, like they say, when it's your own it's different. It's hard enough coping with one baby but with twins it's at least four times as hard. They're like a little tag-team; you get one settled and the other one starts off, or one will take so long feeding that by the time he or she's finished, the other wants more. It's a nightmare. You just don't get any sleep.

But even so, I can't wait to get home this time. They were eight weeks old when I first had to leave them and I knew it would be hard, but I didn't realise it would be this hard. I didn't want to leave them at all, but you've got to, haven't you? I've been sending Julie emails saying, 'It's been so long that I've forgotten what it's like being a dad.' I don't mind being at sea, I've never been sea-shy, but the amount of time we spend away nowadays is ridiculous. I've been away three hundred days in the past year and that's way too much. There's just no let-up.

I've got loads of photos of the twins with me on the boat; one's behind my rack in a frame and I've also got my phone on the side of my bed with tons of photographs loaded on it, and before I go to sleep, I turn it on and go through the pictures and count the days . . .

PETTY OFFICER
ENGINEERING TECHNICIAN
CHRISTOPHER 'BILLY' WETHERILL

A reactor-panel operator, PO Wetherill is trained to operate the reactor in all modes. In a crisis he must quickly restore critical operations and restore this power source to Command.

I wasn't a good lad. I was on a slippery slope, really, getting into trouble with the police. I'd been in court a few times, done for fighting and worse. I used to go on benders on the weekend and during the week I'd be drinking ten pints a night. I can't remember exactly how I did it, but I broke my hand at one point and I've got scars on the top of my head.

Also, I was into weight training and used to take steroids, which give you a feeling of euphoria: your testosterone levels are up, and you're feeling manly, but you can just flip in an instant, and become very, very violent. I'm pretty ashamed of all the hurt I've caused people, I can see it was wrong. It was boredom, I suppose; ask anyone why they're bored, and they'll say it's to do with lack of fulfilment in their life.

I met Sharon seven years ago this July. I was out drinking with the lads one night and she came back to my place for a coffee. The funny thing is, I wasn't going to get back in touch, but then I found her earrings on the coffee table and I thought I ought to tell her I'd got them. So I sent her a text message and then I met her, and that was it. She's a great woman. Very different to me. If there's something to do, she'll do it there and then and if something else pops up, she'll do that too, and she'll make sure every job is complete before she goes to bed. Me, I'll do one job, then have a rest and if there's another job, I'll put it off until tomorrow.

I knew after about six months she was the right woman for me. I got down on my knees in the back of a taxi and said: 'Will you marry me?' I didn't think I was the type of man she would marry, but she said yes anyway. Then we had our kid after quite a long time trying. When I think back to what was going on in my life before, I feel so happy with where I've ended up. I'm married, I've got a kid and I'm a reactor panel operator, which is quite high up in the food chain as these things go. It's a complete surprise compared to where I thought my life was going.

I love my job; I carry out checks so we can start the nuclear reactor up in the first place, I check all the guard lines and that the reactor-protection systems are working, and make sure they are tripping at the correct values and there are no hidden defects. And I'm the person who draws the hafnium rods – hafnium acts like a neutron sponge so the reactor goes critical.

I then manoeuvre and control the temperature of the reactor and try to maintain it within set parameters to stop it going into the red and scramming. If it does scram, I begin emergency operation procedures because if the temperature in the core becomes too hot, there's a chance you could damage it and once you start damaging the reactor there's a possibility of a release of fission products into the atmosphere. We do checks every fifteen minutes: temperature, power and the flow through the core, then every hour I do about twenty checks and take readings from them. I treat the reactor with respect, because if you become blasé about it, it could bite you on the backside.

The future, possibly, is another nine years in the Navy. It all depends on the situation at home. The wife finds it difficult when I go away and if she wants me to pack it in then I will leave. But what I'd like to do is serve twenty-two years, collect my pension and then get a job where I'm not spending so much time away from home.

A SHORT SUBMARINE HISTORY

When looking at the evolution of the submarine, one has a number of different places to start. Legend has it that Alexander the Great descended in a glass diving bell into the Aegean Sea in 332 BC near the Phoenician city of Tyre, and sixteen centuries later Leonardo da Vinci drew a primitive submersible boat of wooden frame design covered in goatskins, with oars providing propulsion through waterproof sweeps, although his plans never left the drawing board. In an era when Europe was consumed by wars, da Vinci could not justify bringing to life what he could see would be a devastating fighting machine. He destroyed his sketches and designs.

Development began to get more viable with a British contribution in the late 1500s, when William Bourne, a carpenter and mathematician, proposed a completely enclosed boat that could be submerged and rowed under-water. It consisted of a wooden frame covered with waterproof leather and included a double-hull construction as well as ballast and trim systems, which are the same principles used today.

The first concept for a military submarine came from a Dutch inventor, Cornelius van Drebbel, who had moved to England in 1604 at the invitation of King James I. In addition to actually building and demonstrating a primitive submersible, he proposed a design specifically created to destroy other ships. Between 1620 and 1624, while working for the Royal Navy, he successfully manoeuvred his craft to depths of up to fifteen feet beneath the surface of the Thames. His submarine regularly stayed submerged for three hours or more and could travel from Westminster to Greenwich and back. James I was so intrigued by this concept that he went aboard the craft and, watched by several thousand Londoners, who lined the banks of the Thames, spent eight minutes under the water.

A number of submarine boats were conceived in the early years of the eighteenth century. By 1727, no fewer than fourteen types were patented in England alone, Heath Robinson inventions all.

It was the United States, albeit still colonies in rebellion, that created the first workable military submarines – and tried each of them out against the invading British. The first

American submarine is as old as the United States itself. In 1776, David Bushnell, a graduate of Yale University, designed and built the *Turtle*, an egg-shaped submersible boat that had the ability to sneak up on a ship and submerge itself underneath the intended victim. The vessel submerged by admitting water into the hull and surfaced by pumping it out with a hand pump. Powered by a pedal-operated propeller turned by foot treadle, like a spinning wheel, the *Turtle* was propelled by a hand-cranked screw, operated from within the craft, and had room for just one overworked crewman. The *Turtle* gave Revolutionary Americans high hopes that their lethal weapon could destroy the British warships anchored in American waters.

On the night of 7 September 1776 the *Turtle*, operated by an Army volunteer, Sergeant Ezra Lee, conducted an attack on the British ship HMS *Eagle*, which was lying in New York Harbour. The *Turtle's* torpedo, a 150-pound keg of gunpowder with a clockwork detonator, was to be drilled into the enemy ship's hull and detonated by a time fuse. However, the boring device that was operated from inside the oak-planked *Turtle* failed to penetrate the target vessel's hull. It is likely that the wooden hull was too hard to penetrate, or the boring device hit a bolt or iron brace, or just that the operator was too exhausted to screw in the bolt. When Sergeant Lee attempted to shift the *Turtle* to another position beneath the hull, he lost contact with the target vessel and, ultimately, was forced to abandon the operation. Sergeant Lee soon bobbed to the surface and was spotted by a British lookout, although he managed to get away.

A more substantive advance a few years later was the *Nautilus*, designed by another American inventor. Living in Paris, and financed by Napoleon Bonaparte, Robert Fulton, who would go on to design the first steamboat, offered to build a submarine to be used against France's enemies – the British again. He was suggesting 'a Mechanical Nautilus. A Machine which flatters me with much hope of being Able to Annihilate their Navy'. He would build and operate the machine at his own expense and would expect payment for each British ship destroyed.

He predicted that, 'Should some vessels of war be destroyed by means so novel, so hidden and so incalculable, the confidence of the seamen will vanish and the fleet rendered useless from the moment of the first terror.'

The *Nautilus* was made of copper sheets over iron ribs; a collapsing mast and sail were provided for surface propulsion, and a hand-turned propeller drove the boat when submerged. It was a distinct improvement over the *Turtle* in that it cruised under the intended victim, towing the explosive bomb, or torpedo, as it was called then, until the bomb contacted the target and detonated with a contact fuse.

After protracted delays, Fulton made a number of successful dives to depths of 25 feet and for times as long as six hours, with ventilation provided by a tube attached to the surface. In trials, *Nautilus* achieved a maximum sustained underwater speed of four knots. Fulton (now given the rank of rear admiral) made several attempts to attack English ships – who saw him coming and moved out of the way. Eventually his relationship with the French government deteriorated. A new Minister of Marine was reported to have said, 'Go, sir. Your invention is fine for the Algerians or corsairs, but be advised that France has not yet abandoned the Ocean.'

Fulton broke up *Nautilus* and sold it for scrap, after which it sat on a beach for a number of years, rusting and deteriorating as the years passed. The name *Nautilus*, however, was immortalised by Jules Verne in his 1870 novel *Twenty Thousand Leagues Under the Sea* with his fictional *Nautilus*, designed and commanded by Captain Nemo. Later, several US Navy boats were named *Nautilus*, including the world's first nuclear-powered submarine.

Britain was the last major maritime power to begin to build a submarine service, with the Royal Navy's first submarine, HMS *Holland 1*, being commissioned in 1901. Although comparatively slow to get started, by the end of the Second World War, British submarines had sunk two million tons of enemy shipping. This was at the cost of more than three thousand men and seventy-four of our own submarines. The heavy loss of submariners, almost a third of the serving members, prompted Winston Churchill to say in Parliament: 'Of all the branches of men in the Forces, there is none which shows more devotion, and faces grimmer perils, than the submariners.'

Since the end of the Cold War, when forces monitored and followed the enormous Russian fleet, the role of submarines has been adapted to complement joint operations. Submarines monitor enemy operations and movements, provide coastal reconnaissance, and launch missiles against land and sea targets, as they did during the operations in the Falklands when HMS *Conqueror* sunk the Argentine cruiser the *General Belgrano*. Submarines assisted in ousting Serbian forces from Kosovo in 1999 and, later, were used to launch cruise missile strikes into Afghanistan.

Today, in 2011, four Vanguard-class SSBN (ship submersible ballistic nuclear) submarines provide the United Kingdom's strategic nuclear deterrent and are the cornerstone of UK defence policy. As well as these four submarines – which carry the Trident nuclear missile – HMS *Astute*, the first of the new Astute-class submarines, is undergoing sea trials and will be ready for operations next year, with another Astute-class, HMS *Ambush*, on the way. The government is committed to replacing the Vanguard class in the late 2020s.

The UK also has five Trafalgar-class hunter-attack submarines, designed for patrolling alone in the depths of the world's oceans, to protect the Vanguards if necessary, or to explore what a hostile country is doing. They move at high speeds, undetected, and armed with heavyweight Spearfish torpedoes and Tomahawk land-attack missiles. On a planet that has more water than land, most nodes of civilisation live within a hundred miles of the coast, and there are very few places that are out of reach of the submarines' weapons.

GLOSSARY

AB	able bodied seaman. Lowest rank of sailor
AIS	automatic indication system
Astute-	the Royal Navy's newest class of nuclear submarine
bio	marine wildlife
board	oral interview examination, part of a submariner's qualification process
Bomb Shop	weapons stowage compartment
bomber	Vanguard-class submarine
BSQ	basic submarine qualification
casing	the light metal hull around the pressure hull
Chops	chief operator
civvy street	the world outside the armed forces

CISE	communication and information systems engineer
CPO	chief petty officer
CO	commanding officer
CSS	command support system
CTF	commander task force
dolphins	the badge that represents the Submarine Service. Issued to submariners on qualification, in a glass of rum
DWEO	deputy weapons engineering officer
EOOW	engineering officer of the watch
ET	engineering technician
ETWESM	engineering technician weapons engineering submariner
EW	electronic warfare
Fighting Arm	the Royal Navy has four main fighting arms: ships, submarines, the Fleet Air Arm and the Royal Marines
galley	kitchen
head	toilet
HF	high frequency (sound waves)
HOD	head of department
junior rate/rating	junior non-commissioned submariner

GLOSSARY

Killick	nickname for a leading rate/hand
leading rate/hand	the most senior of the junior rates
Letter of Last Resort	each current Prime Minister's handwritten letter, given to commanders of the Vanguard submarine, which outlines his/her wishes, regarding the use – or not – of the Trident missile, should the United Kingdom be destroyed by a nuclear strike
Matstat brief	a brief on the 'material state' of the submarine, including outlining staff on board, weapons carried and repairs needed/being undertaken
Main Broadcast	internal channel used for announcements intended for all submarine staff
MEO	marine engineering officer
MESM	marine engineering submariner
mess	an area (or areas) of the boat where submariners live and eat
NCO	non-commissioned officer
Northwood	the Permanent Joint Headquarters for planning and controlling overseas military operations (located in Northwood, Middlesex)

nutty	chocolate bars, mainly, but includes other tuck-like biscuits
OA	ordnance artificer
PD	periscope depth
Perisher	the submarine command course
pipe	a pipe is any one of a number of whistled orders (originally from the boatswain's pipe), or it can refer to the words used after or instead of the pipe's notes
planesman	he operates the planes, like fins, on the outside of the sub, thereby steering it
PO	petty officer
Resolution-	the Resolution-class submarine armed with the Polaris missile was the United Kingdom's primary nuclear deterrent from the late 1960s to 1994, when they were replaced by the Vanguard-class submarine carrying the Trident II
senior rate/rating	senior non-commissioned submariner
Silent Service	Submarine Service
skimmer	anyone sailing in the Navy's surface fleet

SMACS	submarine maintenance, automation and communication system
SMQ	submarine qualification
SSBN	ship submersible ballistic nuclear
TASO	torpedo anti-submarine officer
TI	torpedo instructor
TLAM	Tomahawk land-attack missile. In effect, a cruise missile.
Trafalgar-	nuclear-powered submarine, including HMS *Torbay*. There are currently four more operating Trafalgar-class submarines
Trident	submarine-launched ballistic missile, the UK nuclear deterrent
Type 23	a type of frigate
UAP	electronic equipment used for the interception of radar transmissions
Vanguard-	ballistic nuclear missile capable submarine, of which there are four, carrying the Trident II, UK's current primary nuclear deterrent
VLF	very low frequency (sound waves)
wardroom	senior rates' dining area and social centre
WEO	weapons engineering officer

WESM	weapons engineering submariner
WT office	communications office (WT refers to the wireless telegraphy used in the Second World War)
wrecker	senior rating (normally CPO) whose job it is to maintain, repair and service systems like hydraulics, air, sanitary systems, trim system, ballast system
XO	executive officer, second in command of a submarine

Other bestselling titles available by mail

☐ We Are Soldiers   Danny Danziger   £6.99

The prices shown above are correct at time of going to press. However, the publishers reserve the right to increase prices on covers from those previously advertised, without further notice.

—————————————— sphere ——————————————

Please allow for postage and packing: **Free UK delivery.**
Europe: add 25% of retail price; Rest of World: 45% of retail price.

To order any of the above or any other Sphere titles, please call our credit card orderline or fill in this coupon and send/fax it to:

Sphere, PO Box 121, Kettering, Northants NN14 4ZQ
Fax: 01832 733076   Tel: 01832 737526
Email: aspenhouse@FSBDial.co.uk

☐ I enclose a UK bank cheque made payable to Sphere for £ . . . .
☐ Please charge £ . . . . to my Visa/Delta/Maestro

Expiry Date ☐☐☐☐   Maestro Issue No. ☐☐

NAME (BLOCK LETTERS please) . . . .

ADDRESS . . . .

. . . .

. . . .

Postcode . . . . Telephone . . . .

Signature . . . .

Please allow 28 days for delivery within the UK. Offer subject to price and availability.